日本の神様
Japanese Gods and Goddesses
Nippon no Kamisama

CR & LF 研究所
Creative Room & Life Facilitation lab.

はじめに

本書では、『古事記』を中心に私たち日本人のルーツであり、古来より日本の民を守り、お導き続けてくださっている五十一柱の神様たちを紹介しています。神々の伝説やプロフィール、個性豊かな神々たちがどんな役割を持つのかまで、詳しく紹介しました。

一柱一柱、敬虔な思いを抱きながら向き合わせていただき、その中からさらに神様からのメッセージ（オラクル）も受け取り、掲載しています。

日本の神を知ることは、ほかならぬ自分自身を知ることでもあります。この本を通し

Prologue

The following introduces 51 different Japanese gods, mostly from the "Kojiki (Records of Ancient Matters),"
who have been protecting and guiding the Japanese nation since ancient times.
From their individual profiles to the myths surrounding them and their roles, you will find full details of the individual gods.
We approach each god reverently and provide oracle from them.
To learn about Japanese gods is to learn about yourself.
We hope you will find your own self and feel the connection with the gods in a new light.
And may this book bring light and inspiration to your life.

May the gods grant blessings to you all.
Creative Room & Life Facilitation lab.
Tsukine

神々のご加護と恵みをあなたに。
…………
CR&LF研究所／月音

て、自分自身、そして神々とのつながりを再認識し、あなたのこれからの人生に、光とヒントをもたらすような体験となれば幸いです。

日本の神様

はじめに　Prologue ―― 2

【本編】Main Story

- 01　天之御中主神 あめのみなかぬしのかみ　Amenominakanushi ―― 8
- 02　高御産巣日神 たかみむすひのかみ　Takamimusuhi ―― 10
- 03　神産巣日神 かみむすひのかみ　kamimusuhi ―― 12
- 04　天之常立神 あめのとこたちのかみ　Amenotokotachi ―― 14
- 05　国之常立神 くにのとこたちのかみ　Kuninotokotachi ―― 16
- 06　伊邪那岐命 いざなぎのみこと　Izanagi ―― 18
- 07　伊邪那美命 いざなみのみこと　Izanami ―― 20
- 08　大山津見神 おおやまつみのかみ　Ooyamatsumi ―― 22
- 09　火之迦具土神 ひのかぐつちのかみ　Hinokagutsuchi ―― 24
- 10　和久産巣日神 わくむすひのかみ　Wakumusuhi ―― 26
- 11　宇迦之御魂神 うかのみたまのかみ　Ukanomitama ―― 28
- 12　住吉三神 すみよしさんじん　Sumiyoshisanjin ―― 30
- 13　天照大御神 あまてらすおおみかみ　Amaterasu ―― 32
- 14　月読命 つくよみのみこと　Tsukuyomi ―― 34
- 15　建速須佐之男命 たけはやすさのおのみこと　Takehayasusanoo ―― 36
- 16　宗像三神 むなかたさんじん　Munakatasanjin ―― 38
- 17　思金神 おもいかねのかみ　Omoikane ―― 40

もくじ

- 18 ― 天宇受売命 あめのうずめのみこと　Amenouzume ― 42
- 19 ― 天手力男神 あめのたぢからおのかみ　Amenotajikarao ― 44
- 20 ― 天児屋命 あめのこやねのみこと　Amenokoyane ― 46
- 21 ― 布刀玉命 ふとだまのみこと　Futodama ― 48
- 22 ― 伊斯許理度売命 いしこりどめのみこと　Ishikoridome ― 50
- 23 ― 天津麻羅 あまつまら　Amatsumara ― 52
- 24 ― 大宜都比売神 おおげつひめのかみ　Oogetsuhime ― 54
- 25 ― 足名椎神・手名椎神 あしなづちのかみ・てなづちのかみ　Ashinazuchi/Tenazuchi ― 56
- 26 ― 櫛名田比売 くしなだひめ　Kushinadahime ― 58
- 27 ― 大国主神 おおくにぬしのかみ　Ookuninushi ― 60
- 28 ― 八上比売 やがみひめ　Yagamihime ― 62
- 29 ― 須勢理毘売命 すせりびめのみこと　Suseribime ― 64
- 30 ― 少名毘古那神 すくなびこなのかみ　Sukunabikona ― 66
- 31 ― 幸魂・奇魂 さきみたま・くしみたま　Sakimitama/Kushimitama ― 68
- 32 ― 淤美豆奴神 おみずぬのかみ　Omizunu ― 70
- 33 ― 正勝吾勝勝速日天之忍穂耳命 まさかつあかつかちはやひあめのおしほみみのみこと　Amenooshihomimi ― 72
- 34 ― 天之菩卑能命 あめのほひのみこと　Amenohohi ― 74
- 35 ― 建御雷之男神 たけみかづちのおのかみ　Takemikazuchi ― 76
- 36 ― 事代主神 ことしろぬしのかみ　Kotoshironushi ― 78

37	建御名方神 たけみなかたのかみ	Takeminakata — 80
38	邇邇芸命 にニぎのみこと	Ninigi — 82
39	三種の神器 さんしゅのじんぎ	Sanshunojingi — 84
40	猿田毘古神 さるたびこのかみ	Sarutabiko — 86
41	木花之佐久夜毘売 このはなのさくやびめ	Konohananosakuyabime — 88
42	石長比売 いわながひめ	Iwanagahime — 90
43	山幸彦 やまさちひこ	Yamasachihiko — 92
44	海幸彦 うみさちひこ	Umisachihiko — 94
45	豊玉毘売命 とよたまびめのみこと	Toyotamabime — 96
46	玉依毘売命 たまよりびめのみこと	Tamayoribime — 98
47	神倭伊波礼琵古命 かんやまといわれびこのみこと	Jinmu — 100
48	塩椎神 しおつちのかみ	Shiotsuchi — 102
49	綿津見神 わたつみのかみ	Watatsumi — 104
50	富登多多良伊須須岐比売命 ほとたたらいすすぎひめのみこと	Hototataraisusugihime — 106
51	八咫烏 やたがらす	Yatagarasu — 108

【附録】Appendix

索引　Index — 110

系図　Relationship Diagram — 118

日本の神様
Nippon no Kamisama

本編
【Main Story】

天之御中主神

Amenominakanushi

01

◎守護分野
鎮護国家

◎キーワード
全てを包む

◎ Area of Guardianship
Protection of the state

◎ Keywords
Embrace everything

宇宙の中心に存在する根源の神

天之御中主神は「天の中央に位置する主君」の意味を持つ根源の神です。

『古事記』に「天地初めて、発けし時、高天原に成れる神の名は天之御中主神」という記述があり、まだ天と地が分かれていなかった頃、澄んだものは上の方にのぼり、淀んだものは下の方に溜まっていたとされます。やがて天地が分かれはじめた頃、できたばかりの高天原に生まれた最初の神が、この天之御中主神でした。

天之御中主神は、最高神とされながらも『古事記』の中にたった一行の記述しかありません。あまりに崇高すぎてほとんど生活に関係してこないため、主祭神としている神社はかなりの少数です。

時間や空間、事象など全てを包括する宇宙のような無限の存在で、私たちの存在や生命などの全てはひとつの源から生まれたことを教えています。

The origin of the god
at the center of the universe

AMENOMINAKANUSHI is the original god whose name means "Master of the August Center of Heaven."
As described in the "Kojiki (Record of Ancient Matters)," "When heaven and earth were first divided, the name of the god that appeared in "Takamagahara (Plain of High Heaven)" first was AMENOMINAKANUSHI." Before heaven and earth were divided, the clear part rose up above and the stagnant part accumulated below.
In the course of time, once heaven and earth had begun to separate, the first god to come into being on the newly-formed Plain of High Heaven was AMENOMINAKANUSHI.
Even though AMENOMINAKANUSHI is said to be the supreme god, it is only mentioned in one line of the "Kojiki."
Since it is so sublime and doesn't have much to do with people's lives, only a few shrines worship it as their main deity.
It is like the infinite universe embracing everything such as time, space, and events and teaches us that all of our existence and lives originated from a single source.

☀ Oracle
わたしはすべて。
わたしはただそこに存在し、循環しています。
あなたを曇らせ循環を遮るもの、
それは恐れや固定観念といった古い幻影です。
いま、この変化のときに備えて、
すべての恐れや古い観念を手放してください。

I am all. I simply exist and cycle.
What clouds you and blocks your cycle are the old illusions of fear and stereotypes.
Now, let go of all old ideas, in this time of change.

02 高御産巣日神
たかみむすひのかみ

Takamimusuhi

◎守護分野
創造、むすんでまとめる

◎キーワード
創造と光

◎ Area of Guardianship
Creation, tying and bringing together

◎ Keywords
Creation and light

神聖で偉大な生成の霊力を司る神

高御産巣日神(たかみむすひのかみ)は、「生産・生成」、「日・火」の意味を持つ創造と生成力の神です。地を象徴し女神的要素を持つ神産巣日神(かみむすひのかみ)と一対をなし、地を象徴する生成神、神産巣日神に対し、天上を象徴し生命エネルギーを司り、森羅万象全ての創造に関わっています。

『古事記』では、天地開闢(てんちかいびゃく)の際、最初に天之御中主神(あめのみなかぬしのかみ)が現れ、その後に神産巣日神と共に高天原(たかまのはら)に出現したのが高御産巣日神で、天之御中主神、神産巣日神と共に造化三神(ぞうかさんしん)の一柱とされています。

神話の中では、天照大御神(あまてらすおおみかみ)と共に「天孫降臨(てんそんこうりん)」など高天原の重大事を指揮、補佐する立場で登場する重要神として知られています。

The god of holy and great power of generation

TAKAMIMUSUHI is the god of creation and formation whose name means "production/formation" and "sun/fire." Forming a pair with KAMIMUSUHI, and symbolizes the earth and the element of the goddess, it is the symbol of the heavens and responsible for the life energy, and is engaged in the creation of the universe.

According to the "Kojiki," AMENOMINAKANUSHI first came into being in the Plain of High Heaven at the time of the creation of heaven and earth, and then appeared TAKAMIMUSUHI together with KAMIMUSUHI. Together these three gods are collectively called "Zoka sanshin (three gods of creation)." In Japanese mythology, TAKAMIMUSUHI is known as an important god who directs and assists with the major events in the Plain of High Heaven such as "Tensonkorin (the descent to earth of the grandson of the sun goddess)" along with AMATERASU.

☀ Oracle

わたしはすべてを創造するもの。創造の羅針盤。
光に気づき、純粋な宇宙のエッセンスである
あなた自身に還ることを助けます。
心の中に溜め込んでいる感情のゴミをすべて手放し、
勇気を持って大いなる一歩を踏み出しましょう。

I am a creator of all. The compass of creation.
I support you being awakened to the light and going back to being yourself, the pure essence of the universe.
Let go of all your pent-up feelings and have the courage to take a great step forward.

03

神産巣日神
Kamimusuhi
かみむすひのかみ

◎守護分野
創造、むすんでまとめる

◎キーワード
生成力

◎ Area of Guardianship
Creation, tying and bringing together

◎ Keywords
Generative power

造化三神のうち唯一の女神？

神産巣日神は、「新たなものを生み生成する不思議な力」という意味を持つ、天地の生成に関わる神です。

天地開闢のとき高天原に出現した、造化三神の一柱とされています。高御産巣日神とは共に「創造」を担う一対の神で、神産巣日神は「地」（陰）を象徴ですが、高御産巣日神は「天」（陽）の象徴。夫婦ではなく単独で成る独神ですが、造化三神の中でこの神だけが女神であるとする説もあります。

神産巣日神の司る「生成力」は、「蘇生」や「復活」とも大きな関係があります。後に登場する国造りの神、大国主神が兄神らによって殺されたとき、二神を遣わせて蘇生させたといわれます。

The only goddess of "Zoka sanshin" (three gods of creation)

KAMIMUSUHI is the god of the creation of heaven and earth whose name means "the mysterious power of producing and generating something new." It is known as one of the "Zoka sanshin (three gods of creation)" who appeared in the Plain of High Heaven at the time of the creation of heaven and earth. Together with TAKAMIMUSUHI, the pair of gods is in charge of creation. TAKAMIMUSUHI is the symbol of the heaven (yang) and KAMIMUSUI is the symbol of earth (yin). Although they are not a couple and each are said to be genderless "hitorigami (god without gender,)" some say KAMIMUSUHI is the only goddess of "Zoka sanshin."

Their powers are connected with "resurrection" and "recovery." It is said that when OOKUNINUSHI was killed by his brothers, KAMIMUSUHI sent two gods to revive him.

☀Oracle
死は再生の一過程です。
もしいま自分自身を完全に生きていないと感じているなら、
勇気を持ってあなたが抱え込んでしまったすべてを手放し、
大きな宇宙の流れに飛び込んでください。
勇気、信頼、愛こそがあなたを蘇らせる、
最高の特効薬です。

Death is a process of rebirth.

If you feel that you're not living your life to the fullest,

have the courage to let go of everything

and flow into the great universe.

The best remedies for your recovery are courage,

trust and love.

天之常立神

04

あめのとこたちのかみ

Amenotokotachi

◎ 守護分野
鎮護国家

◎ キーワード
小さな動機

◎ Area of Guardianship
Protection of the state

◎ Keywords
Small motivation

宇宙の恒常性を表し、天の礎となる神

天之常立神は、「大地の出現を讃え、永遠の安定を願う」の意を持つ、天の恒常性を表した神です。天地開闢の際、別天神の五柱の最後に現れた独神で、国土形成の根源神といわれる国之常立神と対になる神とされています。「地」を司る国之常立神に対し、天之常立神は「天」を司っていて、高天原の守護神であるともいわれます。

天之常立神は、宇宙が誕生し、天と地がまだもやもやしていた頃に登場し、天（高天原）を固定して恒久的に神々が住む場所としました。

その働きからこの神は、万物を生成する際の霊妙な働き（物理的なエネルギー）を象徴し、地球を含む宇宙全体を守る役割を担っている神ともいえましょう。

The god of the foundation of heaven, constancy of the universe

AMENOTOKOTACHI is the god of constancy of the universe whose name means "praise the appearance of the earth and wish for eternal stability." It was the last "hitorigami" of the five Kotoamatsukami to appear at the time of the creation of heaven and earth and was the counterpart of KUNINOTOKOTACHI, the god of the formation of the land. While KUNINOTOKOTACHI is involved with the earth, AMENOTOKOTACHI is involved with the heavens and is said to be the guardian of the Plain of High Heaven.

AMENOTOKOTACHI appeared at the time of the birth of the universe before heaven and earth were divided. It secured the Plain of High Heaven as the gods' permanent home. Thus, it symbolizes the slightest movements (physical energy) that produce all the things in the universe and plays an important role in guarding the whole universe, including our planet earth.

☀ Oracle
あなたの中に宿る、
精妙な心の動きを見逃さないでください。
いま、あなたは本当の自分自身を生き、
望む人生をこの地上で展開させるべきときを迎えています。
あなたの中で芽吹いている、小さな動機に光をあて、
それをしっかりと認識してください。

Don't overlook the slightest movement of your mind.
You are now at the time when you should live your true self
and develop the life you want upon this earth.
Shed light on the small motivation germinating
within you and acknowledge its significance.

05 国之常立神

Kuninotokotachi

くにのとこたちのかみ

◎守護分野
鎮護国家、国土形成

◎キーワード
真実を貫く

◎ Area of Guardianship
Protection of the state, formation of the land

◎ Keywords
Holding on to the truth

大地そのものを神格化した神

国之常立神は、「国の床の出現」または「国が永久に立ち続ける」といった意味を持つ国土形成の神です。天地開闢の際に出現し、天地が分かれはじめた頃に地上に葦のようなものが生まれ、それが国之常立神になりました。

宇宙が誕生し、国土がまだ混沌とした状態のときに登場し、泥土を凝集させて生命が宿る大地を造ったとされています。

『古事記』では、神世七代の一番目に現れた独神で、別天神の最後の天之常立神と対をなし、「地」（国土）を司り、国土が永久に成立したことを現す神として知られています。

世にはじめて生まれた神であるともされ、天之常立神よりも古くから信仰されていました。

Deification of the earth

KUNINOTOKOTACHI is the god of the formation of the land whose name means "the appearance of a national land" or "the nation will remain standing forever.' When heaven and earth had begun to separate, a reed-like grass was born which became KUNINOTOKOTACHI. It appeared at the time of the birth of the universe when the nation was still in chaos and condensed the mud to create the earth where life could dwell. According to the "Kojiki," KUNINOTOKOTACHI was the first god to appear of the Kamiyonanayo (seven generations of the gods' world,) and was the counterpart of AMENOTOKOTACHI, the last of the Kotoamatsukami. It is involved with the earth (nation) and is known as the god who proves the eternal nation land. It was said to be the first god to come into being and has been worshiped longer than AMENOTOKOTACHI.

※Oracle
あなたがこの時代、
地上に降り立ったことには意味があります。
自分の中に潜む使命感や真実が、
まだおぼろげなものだとしても、
迷わずそれを表現する努力をしてください。
だれかのドラマでなく、あなた自身のドラマを
生きるために生まれてきたのです。

There is a reason that you have landed on this earth
in this age. Even though the vocation and
truth that exist deep inside you may still be vague,
strive to express them without hesitation.
You were born to live your own drama,
not the drama of others.

伊邪那岐命 Izanagi

06

PAGE 18 / 19

◎守護分野
鎮護国家

◎キーワード
言葉にする

◎ Area of Guardianship
Protection of the state

◎ Keywords
Verbalization

国土や自然神を生み出した天空の父神

妻の伊邪那美命と共に、神世七代の最後に出現した神で、国生みを行った男神。伊邪那美命と共に、日本神話の中で一番最初に出てくる夫婦の創造神です。

『古事記』によると、伊邪那岐命と伊邪那美命は天津神々によって日本国土を形造るよう命じられ、天沼矛を授けられました。両神は天浮橋に立ち、矛を使って大海を掻き混ぜて島（日本）を造ったといわれます。まず最初に矛の先から落ちたしずくでオノゴロ島ができ、二神はその島に天下って、天御柱と宮殿を建てて夫婦となりました。その後、日本の島々や国土をはじめ、河川、山野、食物などあらゆる神々を生み出したとされています。

Father of the skies gave birth to the nation land and nature gods

IZANAGI is a male god. Together with his wife IZANAMI, they were the last gods of Kamiyonanayo (seven generations of the gods' world) who formed the land of Japan. And they amongst the deities of creation they were the first couple to appear in Japanese mythology.

According to the "Kojiki," IZANAGI and IZANAMI were charged with the job of completing the land formation of Japan and were given Ameno nuboko (the heavenly spear) by Kotoamatsugami. They stood on the Ameno ukihashi (the heavenly floating bridge) and stirred the ocean with the heavenly spear to form the land of Japan. The first drop that dripped from the point of the spear turned into Onogoro Island. They went down to the island and built Ameno mihashira (heavenly pillar) and a palace in which to live as husband and wife. Then they gave birth to many islands and gods of rivers, mountains, and food.

❋ Oracle
思考という混沌の泉には、
すべての創造のエッセンスが含まれています。
まず、思考に形を与えてください。
あなたの思いや考えをはっきり言葉にすることで、
言霊の力が地上での創造を助け、
それは形を成していくでしょう。

The chaotic fountain of thoughts contains the essence
of all creativity. First, give form to those thoughts.
By putting your feelings and thoughts into words,
the power of Kotodama (words) supports creativity
on earth and begins to take form.

伊邪那美

Izanami

いざなみのみこと

◎守護分野
夫婦和合、鎮護国家

◎キーワード
崩壊と再生

◎ Area of Guardianship
Marital harmony, protection of the state

◎ Keywords
Collapse and rebirth

黄泉国を司る大地母神

伊邪那美命は神世七代の最後の神で、伊邪那岐命と共に国生みを行い、万物を生み出した女神です。神話の中に一番最初に出てくる夫婦神の妻神で、大地母神であり、黄泉国を司る女神であるともいわれています。

伊邪那美命は伊邪那岐命とともに、たくさんの神を生みましたが、最後に火の神(火之迦具土神)を生む際に大火傷をして亡くなってしまいます。夫の伊邪那岐命は彼女を追って黄泉国へやってきますが、妻の変わり果てた姿に恐怖を抱き、逃げる際に黄泉国への入り口に大きな岩を置き、その岩越しに伊邪那美命に別離を告げました。この後、伊邪那美命は黄泉国の主宰神となり、死と再生をも司る女神になったのです。

Mother goddess in charge of Yominokuni (the underworld)

IZANAMI is a female god. Together with IZANAGI, they were the last generation of Kaminoyonanayo (seven generations of the gods' world) who formed the land of Japan and gave birth to the universe. She is the wife of the first couple of deities to appear in Japanese mythology, the Mother Goddess, and the goddess in charge of Yominokuni (the underworld).

Together with IZANAGI, IZANAMI produced numerous gods, but when she gave birth to the fire god HINOKAGUTSUCHI, she died from the burns. IZANAGI went down to the underworld to look for IZANAMI, but he ran away in fear after seeing her, who was dead and cold. As he escaped he placed a large rock at the entrance to the underworld and through that rock he announced his separation from IZANAMI. After that, IZANAMI became the ruling goddess of the underworld, involved in death and regeneration.

☀ Oracle
暗闇や混沌の中で、
大いなる生命を育くんでいます。
夜明け前には、すべてを隠す暗闇がやってきます。
闇を恐れずに、勇気を持って
一歩前へと踏み出しましょう。
いま、あなたの人生には
新たなステージが用意されています。

There is a great life being nurtured in the darkness and chaos. It is always darkest before the dawn.
Do not be afraid of the darkness
- have the courage to take a step forward. Now, there is a new stage of your life waiting for you.

大山津見神

Ooyamatsumi

08

◎ 守護分野
山、海、酒

◎ キーワード
自然と調和

◎ Area of Guardianship
Mountains, seas, sake (alcohol)

◎ Keywords
Nature and balance

様々な自然神を生んだ山海の神

大山津見神は、伊邪那岐命と伊邪那美命の間に生まれました。神名は「大いなる山の神」を表しています。また別名、和多志大神ともいい、この「わた」は海のことを指します。これらのことから、大山津見神は、山と海の両方を司る偉大な自然神とされています。

野の神である鹿屋野比売神と結婚をし、土や霧、谷、峠など陸地の様々な神を生んでいます。

また、足名椎神、手名椎神をはじめ木花之佐久夜毘売、石長比売も大山津見神の子です。木花之佐久夜毘売が出産した際には大変喜び、お祝いに天甜酒を造り天地の神々に捧供したといわれており、酒解神ともいわれ、造酒の祖でもあります。

The god of mountains and seas who gave birth to diverse gods of nature

OOYAMATSUMI was born to IZANAGI and IZANAMI, and whose name means "the great mountain god." He is also known as WATASHIOOKAMI; the word WATA means "the sea." For these reasons, OOYAMATSUMI is said to be the great nature god who is in charge of both mountains and seas. He married KAYANOHIME, the goddess of fields, and gave birth to various gods of land such as soil, fog, valleys and passes.
ASHINAZUCHI, TENAZUCHI, KONOHANANOSAKUYABIME and IWANAGAHIME are also his children. When KONOHANANOSAKUYABIME gave birth to her child, it is said OOYAMATSUMI was greatly pleased and made Ameno tamuzake (sweet rice wine) as an offering to the gods. For this reason he is also known as Sakatokeno kami, the god of sake.

※Oracle
あなたは疲れ過ぎて
調和とゆとりを欠いてはいませんか？
忙しすぎて、自分らしさを忘れてしまうときは、山や海、
公園などに行き、自然の調和の中で過ごしてみましょう。
自然体の自分を取り戻し、
本来の自分に帰ることができます。

Are you exhausted and lacking the balance and time to relax?
 When you are too busy and feel like you have forgotten
who you are, go to the mountains, seas,
or parks and spend time in the balance of nature.
You will be able to go back to being your true self.

火之迦具土神 / 09
Hinokagutsuchi

◎守護分野
火、防火、鍛治、陶器、窯、交通、通信

◎キーワード
浄化と変容

◎ Area of Guardianship
Fire, fire protection, smithery, ceramics, kilns, transportation, communication

◎ Keywords
Purification and transformation

両親を苦しめた火の神

火之迦具土神は文字どおり火の神で、伊邪那岐命と伊邪那美命の子です。自ら火を出して燃えている神で、生まれ出る際、伊邪那美命のほと（陰部）を焼いてしまいます。大火傷を負った伊邪那美命は、これが原因で黄泉国へと身を隠してしまいました。

妻を亡くした悲しみとその原因である火之迦具土神への怒りのあまり、伊邪那岐命は我が子にも関わらず天之尾羽張の剣で斬り殺してしまいます。

このとき火之迦具土神の死体や剣の柄に付着した血、矛先から流れ落ち岩石に不着した血から、十六柱の神々が生まれました。木をもみこんだり、石を打ち合わせると発火するようになったのは、このためといわれています。

The god of fire who tormented his parents

HINOKAGUTSUCHI is a god of fire and the child of IZANAGI and IZANAMI. He is burning with flames, so when he was born he burnt IZANAMI's genitals. This caused her to hide herself in Yominokuni (the underworld).
Out of fury and sorrow at losing his wife, IZANAGI killed his own child HINOKAGUTSUCHI with the Ameno ohabari sword. 16 gods were created out of the blood from his dead body and the hilt of the sword, and the blood scattered on a rock from the tip of the sword. It is said that for this reason that rubbing wood together to create friction or striking an object with a flint produces a spark.

☀ Oracle
わたしは古いものを焼き、
浄化と再生を促す変容の炎。
魂の真実を曇らせる、すべての汚れを拭い去ります。
あなたの中にある罪悪感、恐れ、
古い思い込みをわたしの炎の中に投げ入れ、
手放してください。代わりに癒しと再生を授けましょう。

I am the fires of change,

burning the old and urging purification and rebirth.

I get rid of everything unclean that clouds the truth of the soul.

Let go of your guilt, fear and old stereotypes

and cast them into my fire.

Instead I will grant you comfort and rebirth.

和久産巣日神

わくむすひのかみ

Wakumusuhi

◎守護分野
食物、穀物、養蚕

◎キーワード
悪習慣を断つ

◎ Area of Guardianship
Food, grain, sericulture

◎ Keywords
Breaking bad habits

尿から生まれた五穀の神

和久産巣日神は『古事記』では、伊邪那美命が火之迦具土神を生んだ際、その苦しみでされた屎尿の尿から彌都波能売神と共に生まれたとされています。

神名の「わく」は若々しい、「むすひ」は生成の意味で、実をむすぶことを表しています。和久産巣日神の頭の上には桑と蚕が生じ、おへその中には五穀が生じました。その容姿からも五穀、養蚕の神、穀物の生育を司る神とされ、神社ではよくほかの食物神と共に祀られています。和久産巣日神は共に生まれた彌都波能売神と結婚をして、豊宇気毘売神を授かりました。この子もまた食物の神で、伊勢神宮の外宮にお祀りされています。

The god of the five main grains who was born of urine

According to the "Kojiki," WAKUMUSUHI was born together with MIZUHANOME from the urine discharged by IZANAMI, who was in pain from the delivery of HINOKAGUTSUCHI.
The word WAKU means "young" and MUSUHI means "generation," and thus his name represents "bearing fruit." He produced silkworms and mulberry from his head and five grains form inside his navel. He is worshipped as the god of the five main grains and sericulture, and often enshrined together with other gods of food. WAKUMUSUHI married MIZUHANOME, who was born at the same time as him, and was blessed with TOYOUKEBIME. She is also a god of food and enshrined at Geku (the outer shrine) of Ise shrine.

☀ Oracle
あなたが口にするものに注意を向けてください。
汚れた食べ物や添加物、加工品の取りすぎは、
体だけでなくあなたの精神や魂の毒となり、
思考力や輝きを曇らせてしまいます。
悪い習慣を絶って、
体の浄化を心がけましょう。

Be aware of what you eat.
Consuming too much artificial additives or processed food will poison not only your body but also your mind and soul.
This will damage your ability to think and cloud your luster. Break bad habits and detoxify your body.

十一 宇迦之御魂神

Ukanomitama
うかのみたまのかみ

◎守護分野
稲、食物、
屋敷、商業、
様々な民間行事

◎キーワード
滋養と感謝

◎ Area of Guardianship
Rice plants, food,
homestead, business,
social events

◎ Keywords
Sustenance and
gratitude

信仰の篤い
稲荷大社の主祭神

　宇迦之御魂神は『古事記』の中で、建速須佐之男命と、大山津見神の娘との間に産まれた子とされます。一方『日本書紀』では、伊邪那岐命と伊邪那美命が飢えて気力がないときに産まれたとされています。「うか」は穀物や食物のことで稲に宿る神霊を表し、稲や食物全ての神です。

　また別名「御饌津神」の「ケツ」とは古語で狐のこと。日本で最も数の多い神社、稲荷神社の総元締めである京都の伏見稲荷大社の主祭神でもあります。稲荷神社といえば、狐の像が付き物ですが、彼らは稲荷神のお仕い。またこの狐たちがくわえたり尾に巻いたりしている宝珠は火炎の玉で、釜戸の象徴でもあります。

The major deity enshrined at Inari Taisha

According to the "Kojiki," it is said that UKANOMITAMA is the child of TAKEHAYASUSANOO and OOYAMATSUMI's daughter. However, in the "Nihon shoki" it is said that she was born when IZANAGI and IZANAMI were starving and lacking energy. UKANOMITAMA is a god of rice plants and all kinds of food. UKA means "grains and food" and represents the spirit of rice plants.

She is also known as MIKETSU. KETSU is an archaic word for "fox". MIKETSU is the main enshrined deity of Fushimi Inari Taisha in Kyoto, which is the head shrine of all Inari shrines. Inari shrines are the most numerous in Japan. Statues of foxes are usually placed in Inari shrines since they're the messengers of the Inari god. The sacred gems that these foxes hold in their mouths or wrapped in their tails are flaming jewels that symbolize the furnace.

☀ Oracle
食べ物の中にある精妙なエネルギーに
目を向けてみましょう。
栄養に満ちたよい食べ物は、
物理的な体と健康を維持するだけでなく、
喜びと光であなたの魂も満たし輝かせます。
食べるときは感謝を忘れずに。
愛と感謝は体と魂の滋養になります。

Pay attention to the fine energy in food.
Nutritious food not only maintains
your physical body and health, but also fills your soul
with joy and light and lets it shine.
Don't forget to be grateful when you eat.
Love and gratitude offer body and soul sustenance.

住吉三神

すみよしさんじん

Sumiyoshisanjin

12

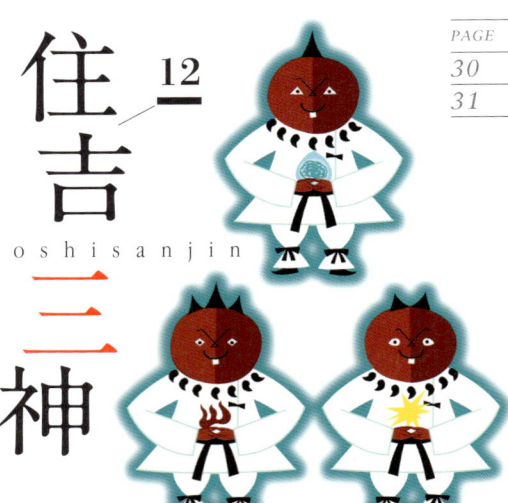

◎守護分野
航海、漁業、和歌

◎キーワード
真実を思い出す

◎ Area of Guardianship
Navigation, fishery, waka (Japanese poetry)

◎ Keywords
Remembering the truth

航海、漁業、貿易などを司る海の神

住吉三神は、黄泉国から逃げ帰った伊邪那岐命が、穢れを祓うために海で禊を行った際に、綿津見神と共に誕生した海を司る三人の神。伊邪那岐命が禊の際に水底ですすぐと底筒之男命が、中ほどですすぐと中筒之男命が、上の方ですすぐと上筒之男命が生まれたといわれています。

古くから航海の神として、特に、朝鮮半島との戦いや貿易において、霊力を発揮してきました。

住吉三神には、現在でいうオリオン座の三ツ星の神格化という説もあります。オリオン座の三ツ星は海上で自分の方角を知るための重要な目印だったため、それが神格化されたというものです。

The god of the sea in charge of navigation, fishery, and trading

SUMIYOSHISANJIN are the three gods in charge of the sea who were born together with WATATSUMI when IZANAGI came back from Yominokuni (the underworld) and carried out a purification ceremony in the sea. It is said that when IZANAGI performed his ritual, SOKOTSUTSUNOO was born at the bottom, NAKATSUTSUNOO was born in the middle and UWATSUTSUNOO was born at the surface of the water.

As deities of navigation, they exerted spiritual power over trade and battles on the Korean Peninsula.

Another explanation is that SUMIYOSHISANJIN are the deification of what we now call Orion's Belt, since it was an important mark in navigation.

※ Oracle

不安や迷いがあるなら、
自分の心の奥深くに潜ってみてください。
心の表面がどんなに荒れていても、
心の底はいつも深海のように穏やかで、
安らぎに満ちています。そこにある真実を思い出し、
再び航路を進んで行きましょう。

If you have fears and doubts,
dive deep into your heart.
No matter how rough the surface is,
the bottom is always calm and filled with tranquility
like the deep sea. Remember the truth that is in you
and steer your course through life once more.

13 天照大御神
あまてらすおおみかみ
Amaterasu

◎守護分野
鎮護国家

◎キーワード
無限の輝き

◎ Area of Guardianship
Protection of the state

◎ Keywords
Infinite radiance

高天原を治める太陽神であり、最高神

天照大御神は、太陽を神格化した神であり、皇室の祖神といわれる女神です。黄泉国から戻った伊邪那岐命が禊をしたときに左目から生まれたとされ、同時に生まれた月読命、建速須佐之男命と共に三貴子と呼ばれています。このとき天照大御神は、伊邪那岐命によって神々が住む高天原を治めるように指示されたとされ、八百万の神の頂点に君臨しました。

あるとき天照大御神は、弟の建速須佐之男命の乱暴ぶりに腹を立て、天の岩戸に閉じこもってしまいます。太陽神である彼女が岩穴にこもると、世界はたちまち光を喪い、様々な悪行が横行し災いが巻き起こりました。困った神々たちは知恵を絞り、天照大御神の気をひくために、岩戸の前で宴を催します。天宇受売命が踊り、神々が一斉に笑い出すと、興味をひかれた天照大御神はつい岩戸を開けて、世に光が戻りました。神事に神楽が行なわれるはじまりといわれています。

The sun god who rules over "Takamagahara (Plain of High Heaven)" the supreme god

AMATERASU is a goddess and the deification of the sun, and is said to be the ancestral deity of the Imperial family. She was born when IZANAGI washed his left eye at a purification ritual after he came back from Yominokuni (the underworld). Born together with TSUKUYOMI and TAKEHAYASUSANOO, they're called Sankishi (three noble children). AMATERASU was ordered to rule the Plain of High Heaven and reigned over the Yaoyorozu no kami (eight million gods).

One day, AMATERASU, growing angry at her brother TAKEHAYASUSANOO's violent conduct, secluded herself in the Amano iwato (the cave of the sun goddess). When the sun goddess hid herself the world was immediately plunged into darkness and various evil deeds and disasters occurred. The deities put their heads together and decided to give a feast in front of the cave in order to entice her out. AMATERASU's interest was piqued by the sound of AMENOUZUME's dancing and the gods' laughter, and she opened the cave door in spite of herself. Thus the light returned to the world. This is said to be the origin of Kagura (sacred music and dancing performed at a shrine).

☀ Oracle

わたしはあまねく世界の創造の光。生命と本質の無限に輝く光です。あなたや周りがどんな風に考えようと、あなたは無限の可能性と光に満ちた、神聖な存在です。輝く太陽を浴びて、あなたが生まれ持った光をいま思い出し、それを輝かせてください。

I am the light of creation in the universe, the infinitely shining light of life and essence. No matter how you or others think, you are holy beings filled with unlimited potential and light. Bathe in the shining sun, remember your innate light and let it shine.

14 月読 Tsukuyomi

つくよみのみこと

◎守護分野
鎮護国家、暦、農耕、漁猟

◎キーワード
二面性と神秘

◎ Area of Guardianship
Protection of the state, calendar, agriculture, fishery

◎ Keywords
Duality and mysteriousness

夜の世界を支配する、月、暦、農耕の神

月読命は、月と夜の世界を支配している男神。伊邪那岐命が黄泉国より帰り、右目を洗ったときに生まれた、三貴子の一柱とされています。

伊邪那岐命は、三貴子の誕生を喜び、天照大御神に高天原の支配を、月読命には夜の世界の支配を、建速須佐之男命には地上と海の世界の支配を命じたといわれます。

神名には月の満ち欠けを支配するという意味があり、また、暦を読むことと関係しています。

古代の人々は、太陽と共に月を観測し、その周期を数えることによって四季の変わり目や、農作業の区切り、魚の産卵期などを知っていました。このことから月読命は、農耕の神、漁猟の神とされています。

In charge of the night, God of the moon, calendar, and agriculture

TSUKUYOMI is a male god ruling the world of the moon and night. It is said that he is one of Sankishi (three noble children) who was born when IZANAGI washed his right eye after he came back from Yominokuni (the underworld). IZANAGI, pleased to have three noble children, ordered AMATERASU to rule the Plain of High Heaven, TSUKUYOMI to rule the night and TAKEHAYASUSANOO to rule the earth and sea.

His name means to rule the phases of the moon and he is also related to reading the calendar. By observing the cycle of the sun and moon, people in ancient times could calculate the changes of the season, the timing of farming or the spawning season of fish. For this reason, it is said that TSUKUYOMI is the god of agriculture and fishery.

☀ Oracle
光のあるところには必ず影が存在します。
光と影は表裏一体。影はすべてを含み、
すべての生命の種もここに存在します。
いま、あなたの中で神秘の扉が開かれます。
そこで生まれた新しい感覚、動機を信じましょう。

Where there is light there is always shadow.
Light and shadow are two sides of the same coin.
Shadow holds everything and the seeds of
all lives exist therein.
Now, the door of mystery has been opened within you.
Trust the new feeling and motivation born therein.

建速須佐之男命

たけはやすさのおのみこと

15

Takehayasusanoo

◎守護分野
鎮護国家、病気平癒、家内安全

◎キーワード
自己への目覚め

◎ Area of Guardianship
Protection of the state, healing of diseases, safety of the family

◎ Keywords
Self-awareness

出雲国を治めた地上と海原の神

建速須佐之男命は、伊邪那岐命が黄泉国から帰った際、禊祓により鼻をすすいだときに生まれた三貴子の中の一柱です。

父である伊邪那岐命により、地上と海原を治めるように命じられますが、伊邪那美命のいる黄泉国に行きたいと任務を放棄。高天原でも乱暴の限りをつくしたために、罰として髪と爪を切られ、ついには高天原からも追放されてしまいました。

出雲国に降った建速須佐之男命は、八俣大蛇の生け贄になる予定だった櫛名田比売という美しい娘と出会い、八俣大蛇を退治して彼女と結婚します。その後は、幸せな家庭を築き、出雲の国を統治しながら多くの子孫を残しました。

God of earth and sea, in charge of Izumo

TAKEHAYASUSANOO is one of Sankishi (three noble children) and he was born when IZANAGI washed his nose at a purification ritual after he came back from Yominokuni (the underworld). He was ordered to rule the earth and sea by his father IZANAGI, but he abandoned his duty because he wanted to go see IZANAMI in the underworld. He had his hair and nails cut as punishment for his violent conduct in the Plain of High Heaven, and was finally expelled from the land.
He descended to Izumo and met KUSHINADA, the beautiful girl who was destined to be sacrificed to Yamata no Orochi (the eight-forked-snake). He killed Yamata no Orochi and married KUSHINADA. After that he built a happy family and was blessed with many offspring while ruling Izumo.

※Oracle
あなたの中の二面性を大事にしてください。
陽気さと力強さ、やさしさや慈悲心、受容性。
これらの美しい側面はすべてあなたの中にあり、
人生を創造する大切な道具となります。
いま、不要なものを手放して、
あなたが持っている奥深さを感じましょう。

Cherish the dual nature in you, and the cheerfulness,
strength, kindness, mercy, and receptivity.
These beautiful aspects all exist within you
and will become important tools in shaping your life. Now,
let go of unnecessary things and recognize your depth.

宗像三神
むなかたさんじん
Munakatasanjin

16

◎守護分野
海、航海、音楽、美術、美容

◎キーワード
意識的になる

◎ Area of Guardianship
seas, navigation, music, art, beauty

◎ Keywords
Becoming conscious

航海を見守る美しき海の女神たち

宗像三神は、建速須佐之男命が天照大御神に対し身の潔白を証明するために行った誓約によって生まれた三姉妹の海の女神。多紀理毘売命、市寸嶋比売命、多岐都比売命の三神の総称で、宗像大社（福岡）や厳島神社（広島）に祀られています。日本の代表的な海の神で、元々は、北九州地方の海人集団・宗像氏の祭神で、四世紀末頃に、大和朝廷から重要視されるようになったともいわれています。

美女神として誉れの高い宗像三神ですが、中でもとりわけ美人とされ人気が高いのが、次女の市寸嶋比売命。仏教の弁財天と同一視され、財宝の神、美の神、芸能の神として信仰されています。

Beautiful goddess who watches over sea voyages

MUNAKATASANJIN are three sister goddesseses of the sea. They were born when TAKEHAYASUSANOO made a pledge to prove his innocence to AMATERASU. MUNAKATASANJIN is the collective term for TAKIRIBIME, ICHIKISHIMAHIME, and TAGITSUHIME, and they are enshrined at Munakata Taisha in Fukuoka and Itsukushima Shrine in Hiroshima. The three goddesses of MUNAKATASANJIN are Japan's leading sea deities. It is said that originally they were worshipped by groups of fishermen such as the Munakata clan, and gained recognition from the Yamato dynasty at the end of 4th century.

All three sisters are highly celebrated as beautiful goddesses, but among them ICHIKISHIMAHIME is said to be of particular beauty and popularity. She is identified with the Buddhist deity Benzaiten and worshipped as a god of treasure, beauty and entertainment.

※ Oracle

日々の感情にもっと意識的になってください。
流れるように浮かんでは去っていく、さまざまな感情や思考。
そのひとつひとつは大きなエネルギーを持ち、
あなたに影響を与えています。心のよどみを洗い流し、
不要な感情を整理しましょう。

Be more aware of your everyday feelings.

Various feelings and thoughts are appearing and disappearing.

Each one of them has enormous energy and influences you.

Wash out the detritus in your mind

and put your unnecessary emotions in order.

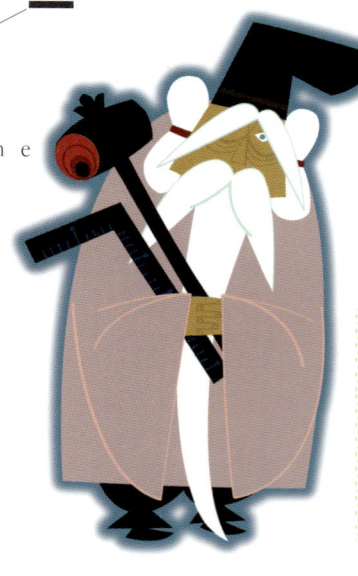

思金神
Omoikane
おもいかねのかみ

17

◎ 守護分野
知恵

◎ キーワード
内なる知恵

◎ Area of Guardianship
Wisdom

◎ Keywords
Inner wisdom

知恵と思慮、創意工夫などを司る神

思金神は、高御産巣日神の子で、知恵や創意工夫、工匠などを司る、聡明で思慮深い神です。

建速須佐之男命に怒った天照大御神が天岩戸に隠れてしまったとき、盛大な宴を開いて天照大御神の気をひき、岩戸を開くために、思金神は知恵をしぼって周到な計画を立てています。また、大国主神に出雲の国を譲らせる際には、派遣する神の選定を行い、その後の天孫降臨では邇邇芸命に随伴しています。

このように、思金神は高天原の神々の中でも格別の知識と思慮を備えた賢者です。力ではなく「知恵」という特別な天賦を与えられた彼は、日本の神々の大多数をしめる自然神と比べて異質な存在でした。

God of wisdom, discretion, and ingenuity

OMOIKANE is a luminous and thoughtful god who is the child of TAKAMIMUSUHI and is in charge of wisdom, ingenuity and artisans.
When AMATERASU secluded herself in the Amano iwato (the cave of the sun goddess) out of anger at SUSANOO, OMOIKANE exercised his wisdom and came up with a well-laid plan to hold a feast in order to catch AMATERASU's attention and get her to open the cave door. He also chose gods to send down with OOKUNINUSHI when he was ordered to rule Izumo. Afterwards, OMOIKANE accompanied NINIGI in the "Tensonkorin (the descent to earth of the grandson of the sun goddess)".
Thus, OMOIKANE is a sage equipped with special knowledge and discretion even amongst the gods of Plain of High Heaven. As he was gifted with wisdom and not power, he is a separate being compared to the nature gods who represent most of the Japanese gods.

※ Oracle
あなたの内側に存在する大いなる知恵が
目覚めるときを迎えました。
自分らしくあることへの信頼を取り戻しましょう。
創造性を邪魔している思い込みや古い観念を手放したとき、
新しいアイデアや知恵が湧き出るように浮かんでくるでしょう。

It is time for the great wisdom that exists inside of you to awaken.
Regain the confidence to be yourself.
New ideas and wisdom will come flowing forth when you let go
of the stereotypes and old ideas that block your creativity.

天宇受売命

18

Amenouzume

あめのうずめのみこと

◎ 守護分野
踊り、巫女、芸術、懐柔、夫婦和合

◎ キーワード
情熱の力

◎ Area of Guardianship
Dance, miko(shrine maidens), art, conciliation, marital harmony

◎ Keywords
Power of passion

天岩戸の物語で活躍した芸能の神

天宇受売命は、天岩戸神話で天照大御神が天の岩戸に身を隠したときに、天照大御神の気をひくために熱狂的な踊りを披露し、岩戸開きに貢献した重要な女神です。神事芸能のルーツとされ、舞楽や芸能の神として親しまれています。神名の「宇受」は「かんざし」の意で、「飾りをして神祭りをする女神」、さらには神懸った巫女を神格化したものともされています。

天宇受売命は天照大御神の厚い信頼を得て、天孫降臨の際には、邇邇芸命に随行して地上に降ることになりました。その途中で国津神である猿田毘古神と運命的に出会って結婚し、猿田毘古神の故郷である伊勢国に住んだといわれています。

God of entertainment who played an active role at Amano iwato.

AMENOUZUME is an important goddess who contributed to the opening of the cave door by performing a passionate dance when AMATERASU had secluded herself in the Amano iwato (the cave of the sun goddess). Said to be the roots of Shinto ritual performing art, AMENOUZUME is worshipped as the goddess of court dance and entertainment. UZU means "hairpin," so AMENOUZUME is "the goddess who does the god's dance with ornaments" and is also regarded as the deification of Miko (shrine maidens).

Gaining the deep trust of AMATERASU, at the time of "Tensonkorin (the descent to earth of the grandson of the sun goddess)" AMENOUZUME was ordered to accompany NINIGI and descend to earth. It is said that along the way she had a fateful encounter with SARUTABIKO, the Kunitsukami (god of the land), and that she married him and lived in his homeland of Ise.

☀ Oracle

こだわりを持ち続けている思考や感情を開放して、
自分の中の知恵やパワーと深く繋がりましょう。
あなたが夢中になれるもの、情熱を感じるものを
探して、それに没頭してください。
あなたが本来持つ輝きや才能を
呼び覚ましてくれるでしょう。

Let go of your picky thoughts and feelings and connect with the wisdom and power within you.
Search for something that can fascinate you, something you feel passionate about, and devote your energy to it. It will awaken the luster and talent you were born with.

◎守護分野
力、筋力、スポーツ

◎キーワード
内なる力

◎ Area of Guardianship
Power, muscle strength, sports

◎ Keywords
Inner power

19 天手力男神
Amenotajikarao
あめのたぢからおのかみ

PAGE 44 / 45

天岩戸を開いた力とスポーツの神

天手力男神（あめのたぢからおのかみ）は、天岩戸神話で、天照大御神が宴の賑わいに興味をもち、わずかに岩戸を開けた際に、重い岩戸を引き開けて、直接、天照大御神の手を取って外に連れ出したことで知られる、力の神です。このときに信頼されたのでしょう、天手力男神はその後の天孫降臨の際、天児屋命・布刀玉命・天宇受売命・伊斯許理度売命・思金神らと共に、邇邇芸命に随行しています。

別の伝説によると、天手力男神が天岩戸の扉を開けた後、その戸を放り投げると、信濃国の戸隠村に落ちました。このことから、彼は邇邇芸命とともに地上に降りた後、信濃に定住したといわれ、戸隠神社の主祭神として祀られています。

God of power and sports who opened the Amano iwato

AMENOTAJIKARAO is the god of power who is known for pulling open the heavy cave door, taking AMATERASU's hand and bringing her out of the cave when she opened the door of Amano iwato after her interest was piqued by the feast of the gods. Gaining trust by this act, AMENOTAJIKARAO accompanied NINIGI together with AMENOKOYANE, FUTODAMA, AMENOUZUME, ISHIKORIDOME and OMOIKANE in the "Tensonkorin (the descent to earth of the grandson of the sun goddess)."
According to another legend, when AMENOTAJIKARAO opened and threw aside the rock door, it fell on Togakushi-mura in Shinano (NAGANO.) For this reason, it is said that after he went down to earth with NINIGI, he settled down in Shinano. AMENOTAJIKARAO is enshrined in Togakushi shrine.

❋ Oracle
神や人間が持つ、真の力とはなんでしょうか。
力は相手や誰かを打ち負かすためのものではありません。
知性や思いやり、愛の中には、しなやかで
無限の可能性を持った
創造的なパワーが備わっています。
あなたの中の真の力と繋がり、
創造性を発揮してください。

What is the true power that gods and humans have?
Power is not for defeating your opponent.
Within intelligence, kindness, and love there is a
flexible and creative power of infinite possibility.
Connect to the true power
within you and exhibit your creativity.

20 天児屋命

あめのこやねのみこと

Amenokoyane

◎ 守護分野
美辞に長けた祝詞の祖神

◎ キーワード
言葉に注意を払う

◎ Area of Guardianship
Ancestral deity of Norito skilled in rhetoric

◎ Keywords
Care with words

祝詞を操り、言霊を司る

天児屋命は神前で唱える祝詞を操り、言葉の霊を司る言霊の神です。神名の「コヤネ」は「小さな屋根(の建物)」の意味で、託宣の神の居所のことを指し、言霊の神、祝詞の祖神とされています。

天岩戸の神話では岩戸隠れの際に、岩戸の前で祝詞を読み上げ、天照大御神が岩戸をわずかに開けると、布刀玉命と共に鏡を差し出したとされます。『日本書紀』によると天照大御神にその美辞を賞(め)でられたとされ、神に捧げる言葉である祝詞のうまさはお墨付きです。

また、天孫降臨の際には、邇邇芸命に随伴して地上に降り、大和朝廷の臣、中臣一族の祖神となったとされています。

God of Norito (Shinto prayer) and spirit of words

AMENOKOYANE is the god of words and chanting Norito at the altar, and in charge of the spirit of Kotodama (words). KOYANE means "a small roof (of building)," which indicates the location of the god of oracles. AMENOKOYANE is also seen as the god of Kotodama, and the ancestral deity of Norito.

In the Amano iwato myth, AMENOKOYANE recited Norito in front of the cave door at Iwatogakure (the hiding of AMATERASU in the cave of the sun goddess). Together with FUTODAMA, he presented the mirror when AMATERASU slightly opened the door. According to the "Kojiki," AMENOKOYANE's rhetoric was honored by AMATERASU, and thus his skill at Norito was recognized. Accompanying NINIGI in the "Tensonkorin (the descent to earth of the grandson of the sun goddess)," he went down to earth and became the ancestral deity of the Nakatomi clan of the Yamato Dynasty.

※Oracle
日常口にする言葉や心の声に関心を持ってください。
あなたが口にする言葉は、大きなエネルギーを持ち、
あなたの人生を創造しています。
ネガティブな言葉を口にするのを避け、
愛に満ちたポジティブな言葉を使い、
望む人生を創造しましょう。

Be concerned with the words you use daily
and the voice of your heart. The words you speak
have huge energy and create your life.
Avoid using negative words; use positive words
filled with love and create the life you desire.

21 布刀玉命

ふとだまのみこと

Futodama

◎守護分野
神事、占い

◎キーワード
心の声に従う

◎ Area of Guardianship
Shinto rituals, divination

◎ Keywords
Follow your inner voice

岩戸を封印した占いの神

布刀玉命は、高御産巣日神の子で天児屋命と共に祭祀を司った、占いと祀の神です。天岩戸隠れのときには、榊を抜き取り、これに三種の神器の一つである八尺瓊勾玉、同じく八尺鏡、そして白い布などをかけた大きな玉串を持って、天児屋命、天手力男神、天宇受売命らと共に、天照大御神を誘い出すという重要な役割を果たしました。また、天手力男神が天照大御神の手を引いて外に連れ出すと、布刀玉命がとっさの機転で岩戸にしめ縄を引いて、天照大御神が中に戻れないようにしたといわれています。

天孫降臨の際には、邇邇芸命に随伴し、その後忌部氏（後に斎部氏）の祖の一柱となりました。

God of divination who sealed the iwato (cave door)

FUTODAMA is a god of divination and enshrining and is the child of TAKAMIMUSUHI. He is in charge of rituals together with AMENOKOYANE. At Iwatogakure (the hiding of AMATERASU in the cave of the sun goddess) he bore a huge Tamagushi (jeweled skewer) made from Sakaki (*cleyera japonica*), Yasakanino Magatama (the sacred jewel), and Yatano Kagami (the sacred mirror), which are two of the SANSHUNOJINGI(three sacred treasures), and white cloth. Together with AMENOKOYANE, AMENOTAJIKARAO, and AMENOUZUME, FUTODAMA played an important role in enticing AMATERASU out. It is said that when AMENOTAJIKARAO took her hand and pulled her outside, FUTODAMA immediately pulled a shimenawa (sacred rope) taut in front of the cave door to prevent AMATERASU from going back in.

After he accompanied NINIGI in the 'Tensonkorin (the descent to earth of the grandson of the sun goddess)," he became the main ancestor of the Imbe clan.

☀ Oracle

あなたは満足のいく本当の自分を生きていますか？
頭でどんなに考えても、本当の豊かさは手に入れられません。
ハートが喜ぶこと、幸せだと思うことを実践してください。
心の声に従って行動するとき、
あなたは大いなる喜びとギフトを手にするでしょう。

Are you living a true self that you can be satisfied with?
No matter what you may think,
you cannot attain true affluence. Do whatever delights
your heart and makes you feel happy. You will receive
great pleasure and gifts when you follow your inner voice.

伊斯許理度売命

Ishikoridome

いしこりどめのみこと

◎守護分野
八尺鏡を作った老女神

◎キーワード
自分自身を見つめる

◎ Area of Guardianship
Old goddess who created Yatano Kagami (the sacred mirror)

◎ Keywords
Self-reflection

鋳物、金属加工と鏡の神

伊斯許理度売命は、三種の神器のひとつ八尺鏡を作ったとされる鏡作部の祖神です。

神名には「石を切って鋳型を作り、溶鉄を流し固まらせて鏡を鋳造する老女」といった意味があり、鋳物の神、金属加工の神として信仰されています。

天照大御神が天岩戸に隠れたとき、彼女を誘うために使った重要な鏡を作ったのが、伊斯許理度売命です。この「八尺鏡」は三種の神器のひとつとなり、現在は伊勢神宮に遷座されています。

伊斯許理度売命は、その後の天孫降臨の際に邇邇芸命に随伴し、天照大御神の御魂代となり、伊勢神宮の内宮に祀られるようになったといわれています。

The god of casting, Metalworking, Mirrors

ISHIKORIDOME is the ancestral deity of Kagami-tsukuribe, who is said to have created Yatano Kagami, one of the SANSHUNOJINGI. Her name means "an old woman who makes a mold out of stone and casts a mirror from molten iron," and she is worshipped as the goddess of casting and metalworking.

It was ISHIKORIDOME who made the important mirror that was used to entice AMATERASU out when she hid herself in Amano iwato. This sacred mirror became one of the SANSHUNOJINGI and is now enshrined at Ise shrine. It is said that ISHIKORIDOME accompanied NINIGI in the "Tensonkorin (the descent to earth of the grandson of the sun goddess)," became the Mitamashiro (spirit replacement) of AMATERASU, and was enshrined in the Naiku (inner shrine) of Ise shrine.

❂ Oracle
あなたの内側の奥深くに入っていき、
心の鏡に映し出すように自分自身を見つめてみましょう。
そこにはどんなあなたが映っていますか？
ありのままの自分を認めましょう。
人と比較する必要はありません。
あなたはいまのままで十分美しく輝いています。

Dive deep inside yourself and look at
yourself as though a reflection in the mirror of the soul.
What kind of person do you see in that mirror?
Accept yourself as you are.
You don't need to compare yourself to others.
You shine beautifully just as you are now.

天津麻羅
あまつまら
23

Amatsumara

◎守護分野
鍛冶、金属

◎キーワード
錬金術

◎ Area of Guardianship
Smithery, metal

◎ Keywords
Alchemy

謎の多い鍛冶の神

　天津麻羅は、『古事記』では天岩戸隠れの神話の中に登場し、天照大御神が天岩戸にこもったとき、祭祀の準備のためにいろいろな道具を作った鍛冶担当の神といわれています。

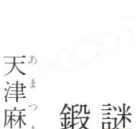

　神名の「あまつ」は天津神を示すものとされていますが、「まら」については諸説あり、「片目」やモンゴル語の「鉄」、「男根」といった意味があるのではないかと推測されています。

　一説には『日本書紀』などに登場する一つ目の神、天目一箇神と同一神であるともいわれています。

　鍛冶は鉄に熱を加えることで、様々な道具を生み出します。頑ななものを熱によって和らげ、新しい創造物に作り変える再生の力を象徴しています。

Mysterious god of smithery

AMATSUMARA appears in the myth of Iwatogakure (the hiding of AMATERASU in the cave of the sun goddess) in the "Kojiki." It is said that he is the god of smithery who created various tools in preparation for the ritual when AMATERASU hid herself in the Amano iwato. AMATSU means "Amatsukami (gods of heaven)," but there are several theories for MARA and it is conjectured that it might mean "one eye," "iron" in Mongolian, or "phallus." One theory is that it is said to be the same god as the one-eyed god AMENOMAHITOTSU who appears in the "Kojiki."

Smithery produces various tools by heating iron. It represents the power of regeneration which softens something obstinate or hard through heat and changes it into something new.

☀ Oracle
熱は大いなる変容の力を秘めています。
心が頑になっているときは、自分の真の力に
あなたは気が付くことができません。
ありったけの情熱を使って、
愛を呼吸し変化を受け入れてください。
新しい自分自身と可能性が
広がっていることに気づくでしょう。

Heat has a great transformational power.
You cannot realize your true power
when being stubborn. Use all of your passion,
breathe love, and accept change.
You will become aware of a new self
and new possibilities unfolding.

大宜都比売神

Oogetsuhime

おおげつひめのかみ

24

◎守護分野
食物

◎キーワード
循環と豊かさ

◎ Area of Guardianship
Food

◎ Keywords
Cyclicality and prosperity

五穀と養蚕の起源となった食の女神

　大宜都比売神は、食物を司る女神で、伊邪那岐命と伊邪那美命から生まれました。

　『古事記』によると、高天原を追放された建速須佐之男命は、道中で空腹を覚えて大宜都比売神のところに寄りました。大宜都比売神は、鼻・口・尻などから様々な食物を取り出して歓迎しました。

　しかし、建速須佐之男命は汚れた食べ物でもてなしたと激怒し、彼女を殺してしまいます。大宜都比売神の死体からは、蚕、稲、粟、小豆、麦、大豆が生えてきて、神産巣日神がこれらから五穀の種を取ったといわれ、彼女は五穀と養蚕の女神となりました。

　また、『日本書紀』では彼女を殺したのは月読命だといわれています。

Goddess of food, the origin of the five main grains and sericulture

OOGETSUHIME is the goddess in charge of food and was born to IZANAGI and IZANAMI.
According to the "Kojiki," after being exiled from the Plain of High Heaven, TAKEHAYASUSANOO felt hungry and stopped at OOGETSUHIME asking for food. She welcomed him by producing various foods from her mouth, nose, and anus. However TAKEHAYASUSANOO became furious at being fed such dirty food and killed her. Then, silkworms, rice plants, millet, red beans, barley and soybeans grew out of OOGETSUHIME's dead body. It is said that this is where KAMIMUSUHI took the seeds of the five grains from. For this reason OOGETSUHIME became the goddess of the five main grains and sericulture. In the "Nihon Shoki," it is said that it was TSUKUYOMI who killed her.

※ Oracle
現実はあなたの信じる思考から創られ、
制限も豊かさもすべて自分自身が創っていることを
知りましょう。いま、あなたの豊かさを滞らせているのは
なんでしょうか。胸に手を当て、
深い呼吸と共にハートの淀みを吐き出し、
光と豊かさで満たしましょう。

Reality is created from your thoughts.
Acknowledge that everything restrictiug your
prosperity is caused by you.
What is inhibiting your prosperity?
Put your hands on your heart and, with deep a breath,
exhale the stagnancy from your heart
and fill it with light and prosperity.

足名椎神・手名椎神
Ashinazuchi / Tenazuchi

25

◎守護分野
親子、稲

◎キーワード
内なる子供

◎ Area of Guardianship
Parents and children, rice plants

◎ Keywords
Inner child

櫛名田比売の両親で親子を守護する神

足名椎神と手名椎神は、八俣大蛇伝説に登場する櫛名田比売の両親です。

二柱は出雲国の肥川の川上に住み、八人の娘がいましたが、毎年一人ずつ娘を八俣大蛇に喰い殺され、すでに七人の娘を奪われていました。そして最後の娘である櫛名田比売も差し出さなければと嘆き悲しんでいたところに、建速須佐之男命がやってきます。櫛名田比売を見初めた建速須佐之男命は、彼女との結婚を条件に八俣大蛇の征伐へ向かって見事に退治しました。

神名の、「なづち」は、父母が娘の手足を撫でて慈しむ様子を表わし、「あしな」は晩成の稲、「てな」は早稲を表すとされています。

KUSHINADA's parents, gods who protect the family

ASHINAZUCHI and TENAZUCHI are the parents of KUSHINADA, who appears in the myth of Yamata no Orochi (the eight-forked-snake). They lived upriver at the Hino river in Izumo and used to have eight daughters, but Yamata no Orochi ate one every year so they had already lost seven. When they were grieving that their last remaining daughter KUSHINADA was to be sacrificed, TAKEHAYASUSANOO came by. Falling in love with KUSHINADA, TAKEHAYASUSANOO agreed to kill Yamata no Orochi on the condition that he could take her as his wife. NAZUCHI represents the way parents caress their daughters' hands and feet with loving care, while ASHINA means "late ripening rice plant" and TENA means "early ripening rice plant."

※Oracle
あなたの現実は内なる世界の反映です。
もし、いまの現実がうまくいっていないように感じるなら、
あなたの内なる子供との関係性を見直しましょう。
親が無条件で自分の子を愛し守るように、
自分自身と内なる子供を愛し、光を送ってください。

Your reality is the reflection of your inner world.
If you feel something is wrong with your present reality,
redefine your relationship with your inner child.
Just as parents love and protect their child unconditionally,
love yourself and your inner child and send light to them.

櫛名田比売

Kushinadahime

26

くしなだひめ

◎守護分野
恋愛成就、夫婦和合、美容、稲田、子育て

◎キーワード
豊かさへの変化

◎ Area of Guardianship
Success in love, marital harmony, beauty, rice fields, child rearing

◎ Keywords
Transformation into prosperousness

建速須佐之男命に救われた豊穣の女神

櫛名田比売は、八俣大蛇伝説のヒロインとなった、豊穣と子育てを司る美しい女神です。彼女は出雲国の肥川の上流に住む足名椎神と手名椎神という老夫婦神の娘で、八俣大蛇という恐ろしい怪物に生贄として捧げられようとしていました。そこへ、高天原を追放された建速須佐之男命がやってきます。

建速須佐之男命は、彼女との結婚を条件に八俣大蛇退治を請け負いました。建速須佐之男命はその身を守るため、彼女を櫛に変え、怪物を退治。その後、彼女と共に住む場所を探し、須賀の地に宮殿を建てました。櫛名田比売は建速須佐之男命と結婚し、大国主神へと続く国津神の家系を築いていきます。

Goddess of fertility who was saved by TAKEHAYASUSANOO

KUSHINADA is the beautiful goddess of fertility and child rearing and is the heroine of the Yamata no Orochi (the eight-forked-snake) myth. She is one daughter of the old couple ASHINAZUCHI and TENAZUCHI, deities who lived upriver of Hino river in Izumo. She was about to be sacrificed to the terrifying monster called Yamata no Orochi. Then TAKEHAYASUSANOO came by, who had been exiled from the Plain of High Heaven.
TAKEHAYASUSANOO promised to kill Yamata no Orochi in return for KUSHINADA's hand in marriage. He changed KUSHINADA into a comb in order to protect her and killed the monster. Later, they searched for a place to live and built a palace at Suga. KUSHINADA married TAKEHAYASUSANOO, and went on to establish the Kunitsukami (god of the land) family who were led to the OOKUNINUSHI.

※Oracle
いま、あなたは豊穣のときを迎えています。
新しい仕事、プロジェクトをはじめるの最適のときです。
心配ごとや恐れ、罪悪感は成功を先延ばしにします。
なぜそれを自ら遠ざけるのでしょうか。
すべての不安を手放し、
新しい変化を楽しみましょう。

You have now entered the time of fertility.
It is the perfect time to start a new job or project.
Anxieties, fear and guilt will delay your success.
Why do you purposely shun success?
Let go of all your fears and enjoy new transformations.

大国主神

Ookuninushi

27

◎守護分野
力、縁結び、薬、温泉、耕、国土の保護、医薬

◎キーワード
自分自身を生きる

◎ Area of Guardianship
Power, matchmaking, medicine, hot springs, cultivation, protection of the national land, medication

◎ Keywords
Being yourself / living your life

大地を象徴する出雲の大王

大国主神は、天の象徴である天照大御神に対し、大地を象徴する土着神といわれています。

大国主神は因幡の白兎伝説で有名です。あるとき、大国主神の兄弟たちは因幡に住む美しい八上比売に求婚するため出かけ、途中で皮をはがれた白兎と出会います。兄弟たちは兎に嘘の治療法を教えますが、大国主神は、正しい治療法をやりました。感謝した兎は「姫はあなたのものになります」と告げ、その予言どおり八上比売は大国主神を選ぶのです。

彼はまた、須勢理毘売命と結婚し、建速須佐之男命から出雲の支配権を譲り受けて葦原中国を治めます。後に国土を邇邇芸命に譲り、出雲大社の祭神となりました。

King of Izumo who symbolizes the earth

OOKUNINUSHI is said to be a native god who symbolizes the earth while AMATERASU is the symbol of heaven.
OOKUNINUSHI is also known for the myth "Inaba no Shirousagi" (The Hare of Inaba). One day, the brothers of OOKUNINUSHI went to Inaba to propose to the beautiful YAGAMIHIME and on the way they met a skinned white hare. The brothers gave the hare false remedies but OOKUNINUSHI taught him the right treatment. The hare thanked OOKUNINUSHI and said to him "YAGAMIHIME will become your wife" and, as the hare prophesied, YAGAMIHIME chose OOKUNINUSHI.
OOKUNINUSHI also married SUSERIBIME and attained control of Ashihara no Nakatsukuni (the central land of reed plains) from TAKEHAYASUSANOO. He later ceded the national land to NINIGI and became an enshrined deity at Izumo Taisha.

☀ Oracle
あなたはこの地上で自分自身を生きることを
選択して生まれてきました。
自分が誰であったかを思い出してください。
そして自らが選んだ人生という旅を
楽しみながら歩んでください。
感謝と喜びを持って道を進むとき、
あなたの旅路はより護られていくでしょう。

You were born onto this earth choosing
to live as yourself. Remember who you have been
and enjoy the journey of the life you have chosen.
When you follow the path with gratitude and joy,
your journey will be more protected.

28 八上比売
Yagamihime
やがみひめ

◎守護分野
縁結び、傷

◎キーワード
謙虚さと許し

◎ Area of Guardianship
Matchmaking, wounds

◎ Keywords
Humbleness and forgiveness

PAGE
62
63

大国主神の最初の妻神

八上比売は、因幡国の八上に住んでいた姫で大国主神の最初の妻となった女神です。美人で評判の彼女は、大国主神の兄弟たちに求婚されますが、結局は大国主神を婿に選びます。しかし、その選択が兄弟たちの恨みを買い、大国主神は兄たちから何度も命を狙われ、その度、母神やほかの女神たちに救われます。

兄たちから逃れるために、大国主神は母神の助言で建速須佐之男命を訪ねて根の国へと向かいます。彼はそこで数々の試練をくぐり抜け、出雲に戻って国造りをしながら八上比売を呼んで結婚。しかし、八上比売は正妻の須勢理毘売命の嫉妬を恐れて、子供を木の俣に挟んで因幡国に帰ってしまいました。

The first wife god of OOKUNINUSHI

YAGAMIHIME is a goddess living in Yagami of Inaba who became OOKUNINUSHI's first wife. Famed for her beauty, she was proposed to by many of OOKUNINUSHI's brothers, but she chose OOKUNINUSHI as her husband. This caused animosity among his brothers and they attempted to kill OOKUNISHI many times. His life was saved his life by his mother and other goddesses every time.

On his mother's advice, OOKUNINUSHI went to Nenokuni (the underworld) to see TAKEHAYASUSANOO in order to escape from his brothers. He passed various trials, went back to Izumo to create the nation and summoned YAGAHIME to marry him. But YAGAHIME was afraid of his principal wife SUSERIBIME, so she tucked her child into a fork in a tree and went back to Inaba.

❋Oracle
謙虚さを大切にしてください。
あなたはいまのままで完全です。どんなに過酷な状況も、
自分自身を受け入れ信じることで希望の光がもたらされます。
あなたを批判したり、苦しめたりする人を許しましょう。
許すことで、再び道を進むことができるでしょう。

Respect humbleness. You are perfect as you are.
No matter how hard the situation may be, there will be
the light of hope when you accept and believe in yourself.
Forgive those who criticize or torment you.
Through forgiveness, you will be able to
continue on your path once more.

須勢理毘売命

すせりびめのみこと

Suseribime

29

PAGE 64 / 65

◎守護分野
勢い

◎キーワード
献身と守護

◎ Area of Guardianship
Vigor

◎ Keywords
Dedication and protection

大国主神の正妻とされる女神

須勢理毘売命は、建速須佐之男命の娘で大国主神の正妻とされる威勢のよい女神です。神名の「すせり」は、父神と神名「すさ」と同語で、荒すさぶ、凄すさまじいの意味を持っていて、勢いのまま進む彼女の性質をよく表しています。

須勢理毘売命は、父の建速須佐之男命から夫の大国主神に対し数々の試練が与えられる中、様々な呪具や助言を与えてあらゆる危機から夫を助けました。建速須佐之男命の国である根の国は、地底世界（冥界）との解釈もあり、その娘である彼女は父同様、魔力に長けていたともされます。嫉妬深く周囲に恐れられましたが、結局は夫婦で仲むつまじく過ごしたようです。

The goddess said to be the principal wife of OOKUNINUSHI

SUSERIBIME is a spirited goddess who is the daughter of TAKEHAYASUSANOO and the principal wife of OOKUNINUSHI. The "SUSERI" part of her name has the same origin as SUSA in her father's name, which means "stormy" or "tremendous," and represents her tendency often to act on the spur of the moment.

SUSERIBIME saved her husband OOKUNINUSHI from many kinds of danger by giving him magical items and advice during the various trials given to him by her father. TAKEHAYASUSANOO's country of Nenokuni is considered the underworld, and it is said that his daughter also has the same magical power as her father. Though SUSERIBIME was feared by those around her for her jealousy, she lived happily with her husband.

● Oracle
あなたが持つ一途さを大切にしてください。ハートに手を当て、自分の気持ちを正直に見つめてみましょう。あなたが本当にやりたいことと望まないことを振り分け、望むことを選択してください。そしてそこに情熱を注いでください。道は開けます。

Treasure your devotion. Put your hands on your heart and look at your feelings truthfully.
Sort what you really want to do and what you do not desire, and choose what you desire.
Be passionate about it and you will find be a way.

少名毘古那神
すくなびこなのかみ

30

◎守護分野
お酒、温泉

◎キーワード
生命と祝福

◎ Area of Guardianship
Alcohol, hot springs

◎ Keywords
Life and blessing

Sukunabikona

大国主神の国造りに貢献する小人神

少名毘古那神は、大国主神の国造り神話の中に登場します。波の彼方から船に乗って来訪した、とても小さな神であったとされ、一寸法師のモデルとされています。

あるとき、大国主神は出雲の海岸で一柱の小さな神と出会います。名前を聞いてもなにも答えないので、物知りで知られる案山子のくえびこに尋ねたところ、神産巣日神の子であるとのこと。その後二人は、神産巣日神に「兄弟となって、この国を造り固めなさい」と命じられ、共に国造りに励んだとされます。

少名毘古那神は、医薬、温泉、石、酒造、穀物などに関わる多彩な能力を持ち、大国主神が病に倒れたときも、温泉を見つけてその病を治したそうです。

Small god who contributes to OOKUNINUSHI's creation of the nation

SUKUNABIKONA appears in the myth of OOKUNINUSHI's creation of the nation. It is said to that he was a very small god who came by boat from far away across the sea and that the Issunboshi (one inch boy) was modeled on him.
One day, OOKUNINUSHI met a small god at the coast of Izumo. Since he didn't reply even when he asked his name, OOKUNINUSHI asked Kuebiko the knowledgeable scarecrow and found out that he was the child of KAMIMUSUHI. Later, SUKUNABIKONA and OOKUNINUSHI were ordered by KAMIMUSUHI to become brothers and form the land, so they worked hard together to create the nation.
SUKUNABIKONA has various talents such as medication, hot springs, stones, brewing, and grains. He also found a hot spring to heal OOKUNINUSHI when he became ill.

☀ Oracle
自然界のあらゆる命は私たちを支えてくれます。
これは天の祝福による贈り物です。
自然界のすべての要素（地、水、風、火）、
植物、動物、人間、そして天にある月と太陽、神、
すべては繋がっているということを知ってください。
あなたはいつでもこの恩恵を受け取ることができます。

All life in the natural world supports us.
This is a gift through heaven's benediction.
Know that all the elements (earth, water, wind, and fire),
plants, animals, humans, the moon, the sun,
and gods are connected to each other.
You can receive this blessing at any time.

◎守護分野
幸と奇跡

◎キーワード
真実を貫く

◎ Area of Guardianship
Happiness and miracles

◎ Keywords
Unification of opposites

31

幸魂・奇魂

さきみたま・くしみたま

Sakimitama/Kushimitama

PAGE
68
69

神の霊魂が持つふたつの異なった側面

幸魂と奇魂は、神の霊魂が持つふたつの側面のことを指す神道の概念です。神道では、神の霊魂が持つ側面には、荒魂と和魂のふたつがあるとされ、荒魂は、祟りや天変地異を引き起こしたり、病を流行らせたりと人の心を荒ぶらせ争いへ駆り立てる神の荒々しい側面を表しています。また、和魂は、日や雨や、日々の恵みの平和的な落ち着いたご加護の側面です。

和魂はさらに幸魂と奇魂に分類され、幸魂は、花が咲く、物が割き分かれるといった、物が分裂し増加繁殖して栄える力を意味しています。また奇魂は、櫛で乱れた頭髪を解いて整えたり、串刺しにして複数の物を揃えるように、統一して調和する力を意味しています。

Two different aspects of the spirit of gods

SAKIMITAMA/KUSHIMITAMA is the Shinto concept of two aspects of the spirit of gods. In Shinto, there are two aspects of gods, known as Aratama and Nigitama. Aratama indicates the rough aspect of gods that causes curses and catastrophe, incites conflict, and makes people's hearts vicious when it spreads like disease. Nigitama indicates the tranquil aspect of gods represented by sunlight, rain, and everyday blessings.
Nigitama is subdivided into SAKIMITAMA and KUSHIMITAMA. SAKIMITAMA means the power of flourishing when things divide, increase, and multiply, such as flowers blooming or objects splitting. KUSHIMITAMA means the power of integrating and harmonizing, such as straightening and tidying unkempt hair with a comb or arranging multiple items on a skewer.

✺Oracle
地上の世界には二元性が存在します。
昼と夜、天と地、女性と男性。そして人の中にも
光と影、思考と感情などの二元性があり、
この陰陽の対極をはっきり見ていくことで
あなた自身を統合することができます。統合によって、
あなたは癒され、大きな変容がもたらされるでしょう。

Duality exists in the world. Day and night,
heaven and earth, female and male. Humans also
have dualism inside of them: light and shadow,
thoughts and feelings. You can unify yourself
by looking clearly at this oppositionof yin and yang.
Through your unification, you will be healed
and undergo a great transformation .

◎守護分野
綱引き、スポーツ、不動産

◎キーワード
バランスの力

◎ Area of Guardianship
Tug of war, sports, real estate

◎ Keywords
Balancing power

32 淤美豆奴神

Omizunu

おみずぬのかみ

国土を広げた出雲の創造神

淤美豆奴神（おみずぬのかみ）は、建速須佐之男命（たけはやすさのおのみこと）の孫で大国主神（おおくにぬしのかみ）の祖父神とされる出雲の国土創造神です。

出雲に伝わる『出雲国風土記』には、淤美豆奴神が出雲の国の狭さを嘆き、国土を広げるためにあちこちから土地を切り取り引き寄せたとする国引きの神話が書かれています。継ぎ足された場所は現在の島根半島の一部とされています。こうして出雲の国を広げた彼は「これでやっと国引きを終えた」といって出雲郷の阿太加夜神社の境内にある意宇（おう）の杜へ行き杖を立てて「意恵（おうえ）」と喜びの声をあげたとされます。それから一帯を意宇（オウ）後には「イウ」）郡と呼び、出雲の一番大きい郡となりました。

Creator god of Izumo who expanded the national land

OMIZUNU is the creator god of the national land, and is the grandchild of TAKEHAYASUSANOO and the grandfather of OOKUNINUSHI.

In "Izumo no kuni Fudoki (the Topography of Izumo Province)," there is written a myth of Kunibiki Shinwa (land dragging myth.) In this myth, OMIZUNU, lamenting the small size of Izumo, drags extra land from far and wide in order to expand the land of Izumo. The added area is said to be a part of Shimane Peninsula. When he finished expanding the land, OMIZUNU said "Finally, the land dragging is done." Then he went to the Ou Forest at Adakaya shrine in Izumo and pierced the ground with a wooden stick and cried "Oue" with joy. Since then, the area has been called "Ou," (later "Iu") and it has become the largest county in Izumo.

☀ Oracle

思考と感情、女性性と男性性、破壊と再生、
直感と理性など、あなたの中でバラバラになっていたものを
できる限り統合してみてください。
対極するすべてのもののバランスを取ることで、
あなたは本来持った才能や輝きを
取り戻すことができるのです。

Try to unify the things that were in pieces inside
of you as much as possible: your thoughts
and feelings, femininity and masculinity,
destruction and reproduction, intuition and reason.
By keeping everything opposite in balance,
you will be able to regain the talent
and luster you were born with.

正勝吾勝勝速日天之忍穂耳命

まさかつあかつかちはやひあめのおしほみみのみこと

Amenooshihomimi

◎守護分野
稲穂、農業、勝利

◎キーワード
真の豊かさ

◎ Area of Guardianship
Rice ears, agriculture, victory

◎ Keywords
True prosperity

降臨を拒み続けた天孫の父

正勝吾勝勝速日天之忍穂耳命は、天照大御神と建速須佐之男命が立てた誓約の際に、建速須佐之男命が姉神の左の髪飾りから生んだ神です。誓約とは「かくあるべし」と心に期して神意を占うことで、建速須佐之男命はこの誓約に勝ち、身の潔白を証明しています。

正勝吾勝勝速日天之忍穂耳命は、天照大御神から葦原中国の平定を命じられますが、天の浮橋から眺めた葦原中国がいかにも物騒に見えたため、途中で引き返してしまいます。その後、建御雷之男神の功績によって無事国譲りが行われた後、再び降臨を命じられますが、この際にも息子である邇邇芸命を代わりに遣わすよう神々に進言し、自分は高天原に残りました。

Father of Tenson (grandson of the sun goddess) who kept refusing to descend to earth

AMENOOSHIHOMIMI was created by TAKEHAYASUSANOO from his sister's left hair ornament when he and AMATERASU made Ukei (pledge) together. Ukei is the act of divination and a solemn pledge. TAKEHAYASUSANOO proved the purity of his intentions by making this pledge.

AMENOOSHIHOMIMI was ordered to rule Ashihara no Nakatsukuni (the central land of reed plains) by AMATERASU, but when he stood on the Ameno ukihashi (the heavenly floating bridge) to look down on the earth, it seemed so unsafe that he came back to heaven. After the land was transferred thanks to TAKEMIKAZUCHI's deed, ANENOOOSHIHOMIMI was once again ordered to descend to earth. But he suggested that his son NINIGI go in his stead and stayed in the Plain of High Heaven.

☀ Oracle
人間関係や仕事、収入など現実の豊かさは、あなたの魂の輝きによってもたらされます。豊かさを受け取るためには、まず自分の価値を認めてください。自分がすでに必要な豊かさを持っているということに気付いて心から望むことを行動するとき、豊かさは向こうからやってきます。

Real life prosperity such as relationships, jobs, and income is provided by the luster of your soul. To receive prosperity, first acknowledge your value. When you realize you already have what you need and act according to your heart's desire, prosperity will come to you.

◎ 守護分野
農業、稲穂、養蚕、木綿、産業、林業

◎ キーワード
我が道を生きる

◎ Area of Guardianship
Agriculture, ears of rice, sericulture, cotton, industry, Forestry

◎ Keywords
Going one's own way

34 天之菩卑能命

あめのほひのみこと

Amenohohi

命に従わず我が道を生きた神

天之菩卑能命は、天照大御神と建速須佐之男命が立てた誓約の際に、建速須佐之男命が姉神の右の髪飾りから生んだ神です。神名の「ほひ」は、「全て秀でる」や「あたたかな陽」という意味があります。

『古事記』では、天照大御神より葦原中国平定のため国譲りの交渉役に命ぜられ、出雲の大国主神のもとへ行きますが、大国主神に信服してしまい結局高天原へは戻らず、そのまま出雲で暮らしたとされています。そして出雲国で、伊邪那美命を祀る神魂神社を建て、息子の建比良鳥命は後に出雲国造の祖神となって、出雲の地で代々出雲大社の祭祀を受け持つこととなったようです。

God who refused to follow orders and went his own way

AMENOHOHI was created by TAKEHAYASUSANOO from his sister's right hair ornament when he and AMATERASU made an Ukei (pledge) together. HOHI means "to excel in everything" and "warm sunshine."
According to the "Kojiki," AMENOHCHI was ordered by AMATERASU to negotiate with OOKUNINUSHI at Kuniyuzuri (transfer of the land) in Izumo to pacify Ashihara no Nakatsukuni (the central land of reed plains). But it is said that he was convinced by OOKUNINUSHI to stay in Izumo without going back to the Plain of High Heaven. He built the Kamosu Jinja in Izumo to enshrine IZANAMI. His son TAKEHIRATORI is said to have become the ancestral deity of Izumo no Kuninomiyatsuko and to have administered Saishi (religious ceremonies) in Izumo Taisha for generations.

※Oracle
あなたが考え、深く信じていることが
周囲の状況に映し出され、現実を創っています。
あなたの迷いはそのまますっきりしない現実を生むでしょう。
あなたの意志を明確にしましょう。勇気を持って
それを行動することで、望む現実を創ることができます。

What you think and believe is deeply reflected
in the situation around you and creates reality.
Your doubt will directly produce an unclear reality.
Make your intention clear. Have the courage to
act upon it and you can create the reality you desire.

建御雷之男神
たけみかづちのおのかみ

Takemikazuchi

35

◎ 守護分野
国土平定、武芸

◎ キーワード
閃きと行動力

◎ Area of Guardianship
Pacification of the national land, martial arts

◎ Keywords
Inspiration and energy to act

出雲の国津神に天孫降臨を受諾させた武神

建御雷之男神は、伊邪那岐命が火之迦具土神を天之尾羽張の剣で斬り殺したときに生まれました。茨城県鹿嶋市にある鹿島神宮に祀られていることから、「鹿島神」、「鹿島さま」とも呼ばれ広く親しまれています。

建御雷之男神は、国譲りが立て続けに失敗した後、天照大御神の命により葦原中国へ派遣されました。彼は、出雲に赴き、波に剣を突き立てて、国を譲るよう大国主神に直談判。国譲りに反対した大国主神の子である建御名方神を追いつめて屈服させ、葦原中国の平定を成功させます。手柄を認められた建御雷之男神は、その後の邇邇芸命による天孫降臨の一行にも加えられました。

God of war who made Kunitsukami (god of the land) of Izumo approve the Tensonkorin

TAKEMIKAZUCHI was born when IZANAGI killed HINOKAGUTSUCHI with the Ameno ohabari sword. Because he is enshrined at Kashima Jingu in Kashima City, Ibaraki, he is widely affectionately known by other names such as "Kashima no kami" or "Kashima sama."

TAKEMIKAZUCHI was sent to Ashihara no Nakatsukuni (the central land of reed plains) by AMATERASU after a series of failed attempts at Kuniyuzuri (transfer of the land). He went to Izumo, thrust a sword into the sea and went head to head with OOKUNINUSHI. OOKUNINUSHI's son TAKEMINAKATA was against Kuniyuzuri, but TAKEMIKAZUCHI cornered him and made him surrender, thereby succeeding in pacifying of the land. Gaining trust by this act, TAKEMIKAZUCHI was added to the members of the "Tensonkorin (the descent to earth of the grandson of the sun goddess)" with NINIGI.

☀ Oracle
わたしは無知という幻想を打ち砕く、大いなる雷。
閃きと直感をもたらし、あなたに真実と行動力を与えましょう。
あなたがどのように行動したらよいのかは直感や
フィーリングが教えてくれます。天と意識を繋げ、
喜びと情熱の力を使って思うままの人生を表現してみましょう。

I am the great thunder who destroys the illusion of ignorance.
With inspiration and intuition, I will provide you with truth
and energy. Your intuition and feelings will teach you how to act.
Connect your mind to heaven and express life as
you wish with the power of joy and passion.

事代主神

36

Kotoshironushi

ことしろぬしのかみ

◎守護分野
託宣、釣り、海、商業

◎キーワード
天の知恵を受け取る

◎ Area of Guardianship
Oracles, fishing, seas, business

◎ Keywords
Receiving supreme wisdom

国譲りで潔く撤退をした神

事代主神は大国主神の息子で、託宣を司る神です。出雲の国譲り神話で、建御雷之男神が大国主神に国譲りを迫ると、大国主神は「美保崎で漁をしている息子が答える」といって難を逃れるのですが、息子である事代主神は「お言葉どおりに天照大御神のご子孫にこの国を譲ります」と、あっさりと服従してしまったそうです。このとき釣りをしていた姿から、七福神の恵比須さんと同一神であるともされています。

一方、全く別の大和神話の中では、葛城王朝の重要な神として扱われています。天皇との繋がりもあり、現在でも宮中の八神殿に天皇を守護する巫女八神の一柱として祀られています。

God who withdrew gracefully from Kuniyuzuri (transfer of the land)

KOTOSHIRONUSHI is the god of oracles who is a son of OOKUNINUSHI. In the Kuniyuzuri myth of Izumo, when OOKUNINUSHI was requested by TAKEMIKADUCHI to hand over the land, he replied that his son KOTOSHIRONUSHI, who was fishing at Mihogasaki, would reply. But KOTOSHIRONUSHI easily gave in and said, "As you request, we will transfer the land to the descendants of AMATERASU." From his appearance when he was fishing at that time, KOTOSHIRONUSHI is said to be identical to Ebisu of Shichifukujin (Seven Deities of Good Fortune.)
However, in the myth of "Yamato Shinwa," he is treated as an important god in the Katsuragi Dynasty. He has a connection to the emperor and is regarded as one of the Mikannagi Hasshin, who protect the emperor and are enshrined at Hasshinden at the Imperial Court.

※Oracle
あなたに与えられた直感の力を大切にしてください。
頭で考えることをやめ、ハートに耳を傾けてください。
あなたが思い込みや思考を手放し、
心を平和に保つことで、天からの知恵や
インスピレーションを受け取ることができます。

Treasure the power of intuition that has been given to you. Stop thinking with your head and listen to your heart. You can receive wisdom and inspiration from heaven when you let go of your stereotypes and thoughts and keep your heart peaceful.

37 建御名方神

Takeminakata

◎守護分野
戦、神風、農耕、狩猟、治金ほか

◎キーワード
弱さを受け入れる

◎ Area of Guardianship
Battle, devine wind, farming, hunting, metallurgy

◎ Keywords
Accepting weakness

相撲の起源を創った神

建御名方神は大国主神の息子で、事代主神の弟です。神氏の祖先とされており、神氏の子孫である諏訪氏などの氏神です。また建御雷之男神、経津主神と共に、日本三大軍神とされています。

国譲り神話では、事代主神が国譲りを承諾したので、大国主神は建御雷之男神に「建御名方神が承諾すれば、もう誰も文句をいう者はいないだろう」と、伝えます。国譲りを迫りにきた建御雷之男神に対し、建御名方神は力比べを挑むのですが、まったくかなわず、降参をして国を譲りました。このときの力比べが相撲の起源になったといわれています。建御名方神は自分の弱さに屈しましたが、今では軍神として祀られています。

God who originated of sumo wrestling

TAKEMINAKATA is OOKUNINUSHI's son and KOTOSHIRONUSHI's younger brother. He was said to be the ancestor of the Miwa clan and the Ujigami of the Suwa clan, who are the descendants of the Miwa clan. Together with TAKEMIKAZUCHI and FUTSUNUSHI, he is regarded as one of the three major Japanese gods of war.
In the Kuniyuzuri myth, KOTOSHIRONUSHI accepted the handing over of the land, so OOKUNINUSHI told TAKEMIKAZUCHI, "If you get TAKEMINAKATA's approval, no one will complain." TAKEMINAKATA challenged TAKEMIKAZUCHI to a test of strength, but he was completely defeated and surrendered to TAKEMIKAZUCHI, handing over the land to him. This is said to be the origin of sumo wrestling.
Though TAKEMINAKATA was defeated by his own weakness, he is enshrined as the god of war today.

※Oracle
強がりを捨て、あなたの中の弱い部分を認めましょう。
あなたが素直にありのままの自分を見ることで、
あなた自身の位置や課題を確認することができます。
弱さや失敗はすべてあなたの貴重な経験となり、
次の収穫の基盤となっていくのです。

Stop acting tough and accept your weakness.
By looking meekly at yourself as you are,
you can confirm your position and challenges.
Weakness and failures will all become valuable lessons
to you and the foundation for your next harvest.

邇邇芸命
にに ぎ の みこと

38

Ninigi

◎ 守護分野
稲穂、鎮護国家

◎ キーワード
魂の原点

◎ Area of Guardianship
Ears of rice, protection of the state

◎ Keywords
Origin of the soul

高天原から降臨した天照大御神の孫

邇邇芸命は、正勝吾勝勝速日天之忍穂耳命の息子で、天照大御神の直系の孫にあたります。ようやく平定した葦原中国を統治するために高天原から地上に降り立った、天孫降臨の神話の主役です。母は高天原の主導者であった高御産巣日神の娘です。

天照大御神から天孫の証として与えられた三種の神器を携え、思金神、天宇受売命ら多くの神々を伴った邇邇芸命は、国津神の一人である猿田毘古神に導かれ、南九州の高千穂峰に天降ります。そして、国津神の首長である大山津見神の美しい娘、木花之佐久夜毘売と結婚することで、文字どおり天と地を結ぶ存在となり、天皇の始祖となったといわれています。

Grandchild of AMATERASU who descended to earth

NINIGI is AMENOOSHIHOMIMI's son and AMATERASU's direct grandchild. He is the leading character of the "Tensonkorin (the descent to earth of the grandson of the sun goddess)" who went down to earth to rule the pacified Ashihara no Nakatsukuni (the central land of reed plains.) His mother is the daughter of TAKAMIMUSUHI, who is the leader of the Plain of High Heaven.

Accompanied by many gods such as OMOIKANE and AMENOUZUME, NINIGI carried the SANSHUNOJINGI (three sacred treasures) given to him by AMATERASU as proof of his being the Tenson (grandson of the sun goddess) and went down to Takachiho no mine in southern Kyushu guided by SARUTABIKO, one of the Kunitsukami (god of the land). NINIGI married KONOHANANOSAKUYABIME, who is a beautiful daughter of OOYAMATSUMI, the chief of the Kunitsukami. NINIGI literally connected heaven and earth, and it is said that he became the earliest ancestor of the emperor.

☀ Oracle

あなたの魂の原点を思い出してください。
あなたは天の意志をこの地上で実現するために生まれてきた、光であり神の子です。地に足をつけ、目ざめた状態でいまを生きてください。心と体をひとつにし、大地にしっかり立って、天の知恵を受け取り、そして地上へ降ろしましょう。

Remember the origin of your soul. You are the light and the child of gods who was born onto this earth to live out the will of heaven. Stay grounded, stay awake, and live in the present. Connect your mind and body as one, stand strong on the earth,
receive the wisdom of heavens and descend to earth.

三種の神器

39

Sanshunojingi

さんしゅのじんぎ

◎守護分野
鎮護国家

◎キーワード
知、仁、勇

◎ Area of Guardianship
Protection of the state

◎ Keywords
Wisdom, benevolence, valor

直系の天孫であることを示す皇位の象徴

天岩戸隠れのときに布刀玉命が使用した八尺瓊勾玉と八咫鏡、そして、建速須佐之男命が、出雲で倒した八俣大蛇の尾から抜き取り、天照大御神に献上したという草薙剣。これら三つの宝物を総称して、三種の神器と呼びます。

これらが三種の神器といわれるのは、それが直系の天孫を継承する証となる宝物だから。三種の神器は、邇邇芸命が、高天原から葦原中国に降臨したときに授けられたといわれます。以後、たびたび歴史の表舞台に登場しながら、歴代の天皇に受け継がれ、現在では、伊勢の皇大神宮に八咫鏡を、皇居に八尺瓊勾玉を、熱田神宮に草薙剣を祀り、それぞれ厳しく神性を守られています。

Symbol of the Imperial throne and proof of the direct grandchild of the sun goddess

"SANSHUNOJINGI" is the collective term for Yasakanino Magatama (the sacred jewel,) Yatano Kagami (the sacred mirror) and Kusanagino Tsurugi (the sacred sword). The first two were used at Iwatogakure (the hiding of AMATERASU in the cave of the sun god) by FUTODAMA and the latter one was pulled out from the tail of Yamata no Orochi (the eight-forked-snake) and presented to AMATERASU by TAKEHAYASUSANOO.

The reason these are called SANSHUNOJINGI is that they are the proof of the direct descent of the grandchild of the the sun goddess. It is said that the SANSHUNOJINGI were given to NINIGI when he descended to Ashihara no Nakatsukuni (the central land of reed plains.) They often appear in historic scenes and have been inherited by successive emperors. Yatano Kagami is enshrined at Kotai Jingu in Ise, Yasakanino Magatama at the Imperial Palace and Kusanagino Tsurugi at Atsuta Jingu, and their divinity is strictly protected.

🌼 Oracle
「知」は、神の知恵。「仁」は、思いやりの心、すなわち愛。
そして「勇」は、正しいことを敢然と実行すること。
天から与えられたこの三種の知恵を、あなたの人生に
取り入れてください。これらをバランスよく使うことで、
あなたは本当に望む現実を生きられるようになるでしょう。

"Chi" is the wisdom of god and "Jin" is a caring heart;
in other words, love. "Yu"is to do the right thing bravely.
Incorporate these three wisdoms from heaven into your life.
By using them in a balanced manner,
you will be able to live the reality that you truly desire.

40 猿田毘古神
Sarutabiko
さるたびこのかみ

◎守護分野
境界、道案内、導き、旅

◎キーワード
真実の道を照らす

◎ Area of Guardianship
Borders, guidance, direction, travel

◎ Keywords
Illuminating the true path

天孫一行を道案内した有力な国津神

猿田毘古神は、伊勢地方に本拠を置く有力な国津神。天孫降臨の際、高天原と葦原中国の境にある分かれ道「天之八衢」に立って、邇邇芸命らを出迎え、先導を務めました。このことから、猿田毘古神は境界の守護神、あるいは道案内の神とされています。

天と地双方に光を放ち、眼光鋭く、背が高く、赤ら顔で、長い手足と鼻を持つその容貌は、天狗の首領とも目されています。猿田毘古神の案内で無事高千穂に降り立った邇邇芸命は、道案内をしてくれた猿田毘古神を故郷の伊勢まで送るよう天宇受売命に命じます。二柱は、そのまま夫婦となって共に暮らすことになりました。

Leading Kunitsukami, who guided the Tensonkorin

SARUTABIKO is the leading Kunitsukami (god of the land) in the Ise region. At the Tensonkorin (the descent to earth of the grandson of the sun goddess,) he stood at the crossroads of Ameno Yachimata, at the border of the Plain of High Heaven, and Ashihara no Nakatsukuni (the central land of reed plains,) and welcomed and lead the way for NINIGI and the others. For this reason SARUTABIKO is said to be the guardian of borders and a god of guiding the way.

With his appearance casting light to heaven and earth, sharp-eyed, tall, red-faced, and long-limbed he is considered to be the chief of Tengu (long-nosed goblins.) After NINIGI went down to Takachiho with SARUTABIKO's guidance, he ordered AMENOUZUME to accompany SARUTABIKO to his home in Ise. They got married and lived together.

☀ Oracle

あなたが人生の岐路に立ったときや迷いで前に進めないとき、わたしの名を呼び深呼吸をしてください。呼吸と共に心の奥深くに入って、正直な気持ちを見つめてみましょう。
ハートが喜びを感じる選択こそがあなたの真実です。
それが指し示す道に、まず一歩を踏み出しましょう。

When you stand at a crossroads or are unable to move forward
due to doubts, call my name and take a deep breath.
Dive deep into your heart with that breath
and take a sincere look at your feelings.
It is the choice that makes your heart happy that is your truth.
 Take a step toward the path that truth directs.

木花之佐久夜毘売

このはなのさくやびめ

PAGE 88/89

41

Konohananosakuyabime

◎守護分野
妻の守護、酒造、山火鎮護、五穀豊饒

◎キーワード
愛と目覚め

◎ Area of Guardianship
Protection of wives, brewing, protection against forest fires, bountiful harvests

◎ Keywords
Love and awakening

邇邇芸命の御子を産んだ美しい女神

木花之佐久夜毘売は、国津神の首長である大山津見神の娘。神名の「木花」は特に桜を意味し、咲き誇る桜のような絶世の美女として有名です。

天孫降臨を果たした邇邇芸命に見初められて結婚しますが、たった一夜の契りで身籠ったため、国津神の子ではないのかと夫に疑われてしまいます。そこで、「もし、おなかの子が国津神の子なら、無事には生まれないはず」と、産屋にこもって自ら火を放ち、炎の中で三柱の神を出産、身の潔白を証明しました。

父である大山津見神は、孫の誕生を喜び、また娘の強さに感じ入って、娘に富士山を与えます。さらに、甘酒を造って祝ったことから、父娘共に日本酒の祖神となっています。

Beautiful goddess who gave birth to NINIGI's child

KONOHANANOSAKUYABIME is the daughter of OOYAMATSUMI, the chief Kunitsukami (god of the land.) The name KONOHANA means "cherry blossom" and she is well known for her great beauty, like that of flowers blossoming on a cherry tree. She married NINIGI after he completed the "Tensonkorin (the descent to earth of the grandson of the sun goddess)." However she became pregnant overnight and her husband suspected that the child belonged to Kunitsukami (god of the land.) So she said, "If this is a child of Kunitsukami, it will not be a safe birth" and, shutting herself away, she set fire to the birthing room, gave birth to three gods, and thereby proved her innocence.

Her father OOYAMATSUMI was greatly pleased at his grandchildren's birth and impressed by his daughter's strength, and he presented Mt.Fuji to her. He also made Amano tamuzake (sweet rice wine) to celebrate her. For this reason both father and daughter are considered to be the original gods of sake brewing.

※Oracle
わたしは魂のつぼみを開く目覚めの光。愛の力であなたを守り、知恵とアイディアと真の勝利をもたらします。美と調和は天の最高の祝福。身の振る舞い方、話し方すべてに愛と美を取り入れ、日常の中に美をもたらし、愛と配慮と知恵を持って、自分の真実の道を歩みましょう。

I am the awakening light that opens up the buds of the soul. I protect you with the power of love and provide you with wisdom, ideas and true victory. Beauty and harmony are the best blessings from heaven. Bring love and beauty into every movement you make and every word you speak. Bring beauty into your daily life, with love, caring and wisdom, and follow your path of truth.

42 石長比売 Iwanagahime
いわながひめ

◎守護分野
不老長寿、縁結び

◎キーワード
人間関係

◎ Area of Guardianship
Immortality, matchmaking

◎ Keywords
Relationships

容姿に劣り邇邇芸命に拒まれた姉神

石長比売（いわながひめ）は木花之佐久夜毘売（このはなのさくやびめ）の双子の姉神です。石長比売は、邇邇芸命（ににぎのみこと）に見初められた妹神と一緒に嫁ぐはずでしたが、容姿が劣ることを理由に気に入られず、ひとり送り返されてしまいました。

木花之佐久夜毘売が桜の花のように華やかな反映の象徴なら、石長比売は岩のように永遠に変わらず続く命の象徴。石長比売を拒んだことによって、天孫は永遠の命を失ってしまったといわれています。

石長比売が祀られた大室山の山頂からは、晴れた日にはくっきりと木花之佐久夜毘売を祀る富士山を望むことができます。しかし、思わずその美しさをほめてしまうと、石長比売の妬みを買い、たたりがあるとされています。

Sister goddess who was refused by NINIGI because of her lack of good looks

IWANAGAHIME is the twin older sister of KONOHANANOSAKUYABIME. She was supposed to marry NINIGI with her younger sister, however he sent IWANAGAHIME back because she was ugly. While KONOHANANOSAKUYABIME is the symbol of bright prosperity, like the cherry blossom, IWANAGAHIME is the symbol of eternal life, like the rock. It is said that because Tenson (the grandson of the sun goddess) refused IWANAGAHIME, he lost his eternal life.

On a sunny day from Mt.Omuro, where IWANAGAHIME is enshrined, you can get a good view of Mt.Fuji, where KONOHANANOSAKUYABIME is enshrined. But if you thoughtlessly praise the beauty of Mt.Fuji, it will arouse IWANAGAHIME's envy and you will be cursed.

☀ Oracle

あなたが築いた人間関係をいま一度よく見つめてください。
その関係性のひとつひとつは、あなたに何を
教えてくれているでしょうか。あなたが出会う人の言動、
そこに映る姿はすべてあなたを映し出す鏡です。
あなたの学びを人間関係の中に見い出し、
真実を探してください。

Take a close look at your relationships
What does each relationship teach you?
The words and actions and form of the people
you meet are a mirror that reflects you.
Learn from your relationship with people
and search for the truth.

43 山幸彦

Yamasachihiko

やまさちひこ

◎守護分野
稲穂、農業、水

◎キーワード
心の真実を知る

◎ Area of Guardianship
Ears of rice, agliculture, water

◎ Keywords
Aknowledge the truth in your mind

山幸彦として知られる神から人への繋ぎ役

山幸彦は、邇邇芸命と木花之佐久夜毘売の間に生まれた三兄弟の末っ子です。山で狩りをして暮らしていましたが、あるとき海の漁にも挑戦してみたくなり、兄の海幸彦に頼んで釣り針を借ります。

しかし、ところが、まったく釣れない上、肝心の針を失くしてしまいました。兄は怒り、山幸彦が自分の剣を千本の釣り針に作り直して謝っても許してくれません。

山幸彦は、塩椎神の助言により綿津見神の宮殿に行き、そこで、綿津見神の娘、豊玉毘売命と結婚します。また、綿津見神の助力を得て兄の釣り針を見付け出し、故郷に帰って、兄との争いに勝利。兄を従え、父の跡を継ぐことになります。

The madiator between Gods and humans

YAMASACHIHIKO is the youngest of the three brothers who were born to NINIGI and KONOHANANOSAKUYABIME. He lived in the mountains through hunting, but one day he wanted to try fishing and asked his older brother UMISACHIHIKO to let him use his fishing hook. But not only did he not catch a single fish, he lost the fishing hook. UMISACHIHIKO became angry and even when YAMASACHIHIKO made one thousand fishing hooks out of his own sword to apologize, he did not forgive him.
On the advice of SHIOTSUCHI, YAMASACHIHIKO went to WATATSUMI's palace and married his daughter TOYOTAMABIME. He also found his brother's fishing hook with the help of WATATSUMI, went back home and won the battle with his brother. After subduing his older brother, he succeeded his father.

❋ Oracle
あなたがいま人生で直面している問題の答えを外に求めないでください。答えはあなたの中に存在しています。心の奥深くに入り、本当の気持ちと対話をしてあなたのどんな心がその現実を引き寄せたのかを考えてみましょう。心の真実を知ることで、問題は解決するでしょう。

Do not seek the answer to the life problem you are facing outside. The answer is within you. Dive deep into your mind, have a conversation with your real feelings and think about which mind of yours attracted that reality. The problem will be solved when you acknowledge the truth in your mind.

海幸彦

Umisachi hiko

◎ 守護分野
漁業

◎ キーワード
エゴを手放す

◎ Area of Guardianship
Fishery

◎ Keywords
Letting go of the ego

44

天孫の御子に服従を誓った隼人族の祖

海幸彦は、邇邇芸命の三柱の御子の長男です。道具を交換しようという弟、山幸彦の提案をしぶしぶ受け入れますが、釣り針を失くしてしまった弟のことは、断固として許しませんでした。

やがて綿津見神の助力を得て戻った弟は、失くした釣り針を兄に返すとき、針に呪詛をかけます。これにより、海幸彦は、次第に貧しくなり、心が荒んでいきます。

さらに、弟を恨み攻め入ろうとすると、綿津見神から与えられた潮乾珠と潮満珠で、干潮と満潮を自在に操作されて危うく溺れそうになり、ついに弟に降服しました。

その後、解放された海幸彦は、九州の南部を治め、隼人族の祖となったと伝えられます。

The ancestor of the Hayato clan who vowed obedience to the child of Tenson

UMISACHIHIKO is the oldest of the three children of NINIGI. He reluctantly accepted his younger brother YAMASACHIHIKO's request to switch tools, and never forgave him for losing his fishing hook.

At long last YAMASACHIHIKO, who came back with the help of WATATSUMI, cursed the fishing hook when he returned it to UMISACHIHIKO. UMISACHIHIKO gradually became poor and his heart grew wild because of this. On top of this, he held a grudge and tried to attack YAMASACHIHIKO. But he almost drowned because YAMASACHIHIKO controlled the low tide and high tide with the Shiofurudama (tide restraining jewel) and the Shiomitsudama (tide flowing jewel) given to him by WATATSUMI. UMISACHIHIKO finally surrendered to his younger brother.

It is told that after UMISACHIHIKO was released, he ruled southern Kyushu and became the ancestor of the Hayato clan.

❁ Oracle

わたしは意識を変容する炎。あなたの内側にあるネガティブな思い込みを、わたしの炎にくべ、わたしの炎ですべて焼き尽くしてください。ポジティブな意識に変成させることで、あなたは心から望む現実を創ることができ、多くの豊かさが人生にもたらされるでしょう。

I am the flames of changing thoughts.
Cast the negative thoughts inside of you into my fire and burn them completely.
By changing them into positive ones,
you can create the reality your heart desires and greater prosperity will be given to you in life.

豊玉毘売命
とよたまびめのみこと

45

Toyotama bime

- ◎守護分野
海、安産、縁結び
- ◎キーワード
心で感じる

- ◎ Area of Guardianship
Sea, safe delivery, matchmaking
- ◎ Keywords
To feel in the heart

山幸彦の子を産んだ異類の姫

海神の娘、豊玉毘売命は、綿津見神の宮を訪れた山幸彦と恋に落ち、そのまま海の宮で三年間、夫婦として暮らします。山幸彦が陸に帰った後に子を身籠っていることがわかり、夫を追って陸に上がりました。

出産のとき、子を産む姿を見ないで欲しいと夫に告げたのですが、山幸彦は産屋の中を覗いてしまいます。そのとき山幸彦が見たのは、美しい姫ではなく生みの苦しみにのたうちまわる鮫の姿でした。

本来の姿を夫に見られたことを知った豊玉毘売命は、嘆き悲しみ、わが身を恥じて、生まれたばかりの子を置いたまま綿津見の国に帰ってしまいます。このとき生まれた御子が鵜葺草葺不合命です。

The heterogonous princess who gave birth to YAMASACHIHIKO's child

The daughter of the sea god, TOYOTAMABIME fell in love with YAMASACHIHIKO when he visited WATATSUMI's palace, and they lived as husband and wife for three years in the sea palace. She found out that she was with child after YAMASACHIHIKO went back to land so she went after him. She told him not to look when she gave birth, but YAMASACHIHIKO peeked in the birthing room. What he saw was not a beautiful princess but a shark wriggling with labor pains. When she found out her husband had seen her true form, TOYOTAMABIME was grieved and ashamed and went back to the country of WATATSUMI, leaving her newborn baby behind. That baby was UGAYAFUKIAEZU.

❋Oracle

目に見える形、外からもたらされる情報にとらわれ過ぎないでください。真実は常に自分の内側、心で感じることができるのです。形や目に見えるものだけにとらわれていると、大切な真実を見逃すことになります。あなたにとっての真実と光を、心の奥に探してみてください。

Do not get caught up with visible forms or outside information. You can always feel the truth inside of you, in your heart. You will miss the important truth if you are tied to visible forms. Search for your truth and light deep inside of your heart.

玉依毘売命
たまよりびめのみこと
Tamayoribime

46

◎守護分野
海、養育

◎キーワード
神聖さを繋ぐ

◎ Area of Guardianship
Sea, nurturing

◎ Keywords
Connecting sacredness

神と人を繋ぐ初代・神武天皇の母

玉依毘売命は、綿津見神の娘で、山幸彦の妻である豊玉毘売命の妹神です。玉依毘売命は山幸彦と別れて海に帰った姉神に代わって、残された御子の鵜葺草葺不合命を育てました。

豊玉毘売命に頼まれ、山幸彦を想って詠んだ歌を携えて養育しにきたとか、出産に同行し、玉依毘売命だけが養育のためにそのまま残ったとか、様々な説がありますが、姉妹は二人で天孫の孫を生み育てる役割を担っていたといえます。

やがて、成長した鵜葺草葺不合命は、玉依毘売命と結婚し、四柱の御子をもうけます。このうちの末っ子こそが、神倭伊波礼琵古命。すなわち、最初の大和朝廷を築いた、後の神武天皇です。

Connecting god and man, the mother of the first Emperor, JINMU

TAMAYORIBIME is WATATSUMI's daughter and the younger sister of YAMASACHIHIKO's wife, TOYOTAMABIME. TAMAYORIBIME raised UGAYAFUKIAEZU instead of her sister, who had gone back to the sea after she was separated from YAMASACHIHIKO. There are several versions such as that TOYOTAMABIME asked TAMAYORIBIME to raise the baby and take poems she had written for him to YAMASACHIHIKO, or that she traveled with her sister for the childbirth and stayed there to raise the baby. The sisters played an important role in producing and raising the grandchild of Tenson (the grandson of the sun goddess) together.

After growing up, UGAYAFUKIAEZU married TAMAYORIBIME and had four children. The youngest among them was KANYAMATOIWAREBIKO, later JINMU, who founded the first Yamato Dynasty.

※Oracle
人からどう思われているか気にしないで、本当のあなたを生きてみましょう。あなた方はわたしたち神の子供で、誰もが純真な心と愛の光を宿しています。心配ごとがあれば、わたしにすべてゆだねて手放してください。わたしは神の愛と共に、あなたをいつも見守っています。

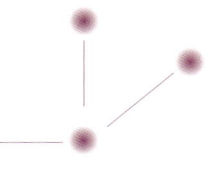

Do not mind what others think about you and live your true self. You are the child of the gods and everyone has an innocent mind and the light of love. When you have anxieties, leave them to me and let go. I am always watching over you with divine love.

◎守護分野
鎮護国家、建国、国家統一

◎キーワード
安泰と成功

◎ Area of Guardianship
Protection of the state, national foundation, national unification

◎ Keywords
Security and success

神倭伊波琵古命 Jinmu
かんやまといわれびこのみこと

〈47〉

大和王朝を築いた初代天皇

神倭伊波琵古命は、神武天皇の呼称で知られる天皇家の始祖であり軍神、穀物の神です。山幸彦の息子、鵜葺草葺不合命と海神の娘、玉依毘売命との第四子として生まれ、大和建国神話の中心人物として名高い英雄神です。

元々は日向国高千穂で暮らしていましたが、塩椎神の助言を受けて東征を決意。軍を率いて、日向国を出発します。

様々な困難に見舞われますが、天照大御神が遣わした八咫烏に導かれて大和の国に入り、奈良の畝傍山のふもと、橿原に宮を築いて天皇に即位しました。

神武天皇が即位したのは、紀元前六六〇年の二月十一日にあたるとされ、今でも建国記念日として祝日に制定されています。

The first Emperor
who founded the Yamato Dynasty

KANYAMATOIWAREBIKO, also known as JINMU, is the earliest ancestor of the Imperial family, god of war, and god of grains. He is the fourth child of UGAYAFUKIAEZU, the son of YAMASACHIHIKO and TAMAYORIBIME, the daughter of the sea god. He is a heroic god highly respected as the central figure in the myth of the founding of the Yamato Dynasty.

He used to live in Takachiho in Himuka, but on the advice of SHIOTSUCHI, he decided to head east. Leading his army, he left Himuka. He suffered many difficulties but AMATERASU sent YATAGARASU as a guide to lead KANYAMATOIWAREBIKO to Yamato, so he arrived in Kashihara, at the foot of Mt.Unebi in Nara, built a palace and became the Emperor.

JINMU ascended the throne on February 11 B.C.660 which is established as a national holiday, National Foundation Day.

☀ Oracle

わたしはあなたに知力を与え、安泰をもたらす創造のエネルギー。あなたは、自らが持つ創造のエッセンスである「知」、「愛」、「勇気」の力を使って、あなたの人生を成功に導くことができます。迷ったときは、わたしの光であなたの進むべき道を照らしましょう。

I am the creative energy who provides you with intellect and security. You can use your own creative essences, the powers of "intellect," "love," and "courage" to carry your life to success. I will illuminate your path when you are lost.

塩椎神
しおつちのかみ
Shiotsuchi

48

◎守護分野
助言、航海安全、
交通安全、大漁、
製塩、呪術、予言、安産

◎キーワード
軌道修正

◎ Area of Guardianship
Advice, safe voyage, traffic safety, good haul,
salt production, magic, oracles,
safe delivery

◎ Keywords
Course corrections

進むべき道へ導く海の神

塩椎神は、天孫降臨や海幸山幸の神話に登場する航海、潮流、精塩などを司る神。神名の「塩椎」は「潮ツ霊」、「潮つ路」を意味していて、それが潮流を司る神、航海の神とされる所以となっています。

『古事記』の海幸山幸神話では、兄の海幸彦の釣り針をなくして困っている山幸彦に、竹の船を用意し、それに乗って海神（綿津見神）の宮に行くことを勧め、航路を教えたとされます。

また、神倭伊波礼琵古命（神武天皇）がまだ高千穂にいた頃にも、「東の方に行くと、もっとよい国が造れますよ」と助言。

別の逸話では、宮城の塩釜神社にとどまり、人々に製塩を伝えたともいわれています。

God of the sea who guides people to the right path

SHIOTSUCHI is the god of voyages, the tides, and salt production who appears in the "Tensonkorin (the descent to earth of the grandson of the sun goddess)" and the myth of UMISACHIHIKO and YAMASACHIHIKO. SHIOTSUCHI means "spirit of the tide" and "path of the tide" because he is considered the god of tides and voyages.

According to the myth of Umisachi Yamasachi in the "Kojiki," it is said that YAMASACHIHIKO was in trouble because he had lost his brother UMISACHIHIKO's fishing hook. SHIOTSUCHI gave him a bamboo boat, suggested he go to the palace of the sea god (WATATSUMI,) and taught him the course. He also gave advice to KANYAMATOIWAREBIKO (JINMU) when he was still in Takachiho, saying "You can build a better country if you go east." In another story, he stayed at Shiogama shrine in Miyagi and taught the people salt production.

✺ Oracle

困難に直面したときは、人生の軌道修正をするチャンスです。あらゆる思い込みを外し、問題の本質をよく見て、勇気を持って変化を受け入れると、新しい道が用意されていることに気づきます。知恵の光が授けられ、その道を歩んでいけるでしょう。

When you face a difficulty, it is a chance to make a life course correction. Set aside all stereotypes, take a good look at the essence of the problem, and accept change with courage, and you will realize there is a new path being provided. The light of wisdom will be bestowed and you will be able to follow that path.

綿津見神
わたつみのかみ
Watatsumi

◎守護分野
大海

◎キーワード
潜在意識と可能性

◎ Area of Guardianship
Ocean

◎ Keywords
Subconcious and possibilities

伊邪那岐命から生まれた海の神

綿津見神は、伊邪那岐命が禊をしたときに住吉三神と同時に生まれた海の神です。このとき水の底の方から生まれたのが底津綿津見神、中ほどから生まれたのが中津綿津見神、水表で生まれたのが上津綿津見神で、この三柱を総称して綿津見神とされます。

神名の「わた」は海の古語、「み」は神霊の意で「海の神霊」。または、「つみ」は「司る」で「偉大な海の神」という意味を持っているとされます。

綿津見神は、山幸彦の海底訪問の神話の中で、豊玉毘売命と玉依毘売命の父神として登場。娘の豊玉毘売命と結婚した縁もあってか、潮乾珠と潮満珠を与えるなど、海の王として山幸彦の窮地を助けています。

God of the sea who was born from IZANAGI

WATATSUMI is the god of the sea who was born together with SUMIYOSHISANJIN when IZANAGI carried out a purification ceremony. SOKOTSUTSUNOO was born at the bottom, NAKATSUTSUNOO was born in the middle, and UWATSUTSUNOO was born at the surface of the water, and WATATSUMI is the collective term for these three gods.

WATA is an archaic word for "sea," while MI means "divine spirit," and so the name means "divine spirit of the sea." It is also said that TSUMI means "in charge of" and "great god of the sea."

WATATSUMI appears in the myth of YAMASACHIHIKO's visit to the bottom of the sea, as the father god of TOYOTAMABIME and TAMAYORIBIME. Because YAMASACHIHIKO married WATATSUMI's daughter TOYOTAMABIME, WATATSUMI helped him as a god of the sea by providing the Shiofurudama (the tide restraining jewel) and the Shiomitsudama (the tide flowing jewel).

❀ Oracle

わたしは、すべての真実と可能性を包括した潜在意識を司る者。あなたの闇に包まれた深層を、神の光で照らしましょう。表面（現実）が荒く波立ち、視界や航路が遮られたように見えても、心の深部にはいつでもすべての真実が存在しています。

I am in charge of the subconscious, including all truth and possibilities. I will illuminate your deepest levels shrouded in darkness with divine light. When your surface (reality) is roughly ruffed and your vision and course seem blocked, all truth always exists in the depths of your heart.

富 50

Hototataraisusugihime

登多多良伊須須岐比売命
ほとたたらいすすぎひめのみこと

◎守護分野
安産、縁結び

◎キーワード
母性と完全性

◎ Area of Guardianship
Safe delivery, matchmaking

◎ Keywords
Motherhood and integrity

初の皇后となった神武天皇の妃

富登多多良伊須須岐比売命は、大和の三輪山の神、大物主神の娘です。神倭伊波礼琵古命（神武天皇）は日向にいた頃、すでに前妻との間に二子をもうけていますが、大和において新たに彼女をみそめ、娶って正妃としました。

彼女は、神武天皇との間に、三柱の御子をもうけます。神武天皇が崩じた後は、天皇の前妻である阿比良比売の子、当芸志美美命の妻となりました。当芸志美美命は皇位を狙って、天皇の子を殺そうと計画しますが、富登多多良伊須須岐比売命は機転を聞かせて子供たちにこれを知らせます。御子たちは、力を合わせて当芸志美美命を討ち、兄弟の一人が皇位を継いで綏靖天皇となりました。

The first Empress, wife of Emperor JINMU

HOTOTATARAISUSUGIHIME is the daughter of OOMONONUSHI, the god of Mt.Miwa in Yamato. KANYAMATOIWAREBIKO (Emperor JINMU) already had two children with his former wife when he was in Himuka, but he married HOTOTATARAISUSUGIHIME and took her as his official Empress in Yamato.
She had three children with Emperor JINMU. After his death, she became the wife of TAGISHIMIMI, the son of AHIRAHIME, the Emperor's former wife. TAGISHIMIMI planned to kill the Emperor's children in order to succeed to the Imperial throne, but HOTOTATARAISUSUGIHIME used her wit to notify her children of his plan. The children defeated TAGISHIMIMI and one of his brothers succeeded to the throne and became Emperor SUIZEI.

Oracle

野山にひそやかに咲く山野草のように、しなやかで強い誇りを持って生きてください。あなたはそのままで完全なのです。ありのままの自分を認め、人と比べることを止めたとき、人生に最高の花を咲かせることができるでしょう。開花するのに必要な情報も自然にもたらされます。

Live with supple and strong pride like the wildflowers
in the mountains and fields. You are perfect just as you are.
When you accept yourself as you are and stop comparing yourself
to others, you will be able to make bloom the most wonderful
flower of life. The necessary information for the blossoming
will be bestowed upon you naturally.

八咫烏
やたがらす
Yatagarasu

51

◎守護分野
導き

◎キーワード
先導者

◎ Area of Guardianship
Guiding

◎ Keywords
Leader

数々の神話に登場する導きの鳥

八咫烏は、神話に登場する鳥の神です。和歌山県にある熊野三山の神使として知られ、三本足の烏の姿をしているとされています。八咫烏の「咫」は長さの単位で、「八咫（やあた→やた）」とは大きいこと、長いことを示しています。

伝承によると八咫烏は、神武東征の際に、高御産巣日神（たかみむすひのかみ）によって神武天皇の元に遣わされ、熊野から大和に入る険路の先導となった大烏といわれています。

また、現在ではサッカーの日本代表のシンボルマークなどとして使用され、サッカーの守護神としても信仰されています。

三本足の鳥の神話は世界中にあるようです。太陽と関連付けられている場合も多く、導きの鳥として神格化されています。

The guiding bird which appears in many myths

YATAGARASU is the bird god which appears in myths. It is known as the messenger of god of Kumano Sanzan (three shrines in Kumano) in Wakayama, and its appearance is said to be that of a three-legged crow.
TA is a linear measure and YATA (YAATA) means "big" or "long."
According to tradition, it is said that YATAGARASU was sent to Emperor JINMU by TAKAMIMUSUHI at the time of Emperor JINMU's eastern expedition. It was a big crow who guided him on the rugged path from Kumano to Yamato. It is also used as the symbol of Japanese National football team and worshiped as a guardian of football.
It seems that the myth of the three-legged bird is found all over the world. It is often related to the sun and deified as a guiding bird.

❀ Oracle
わたしはすべてを見とおす目。天の先導者として、人々の人生に道を示します。道に迷い、行く方向を見失ったとしても慌てる必要はありません。何かの障害にあって立ち止るとき、それは気づきのチャンスでもあるのです。そのテーマをよく見てください。

I am the eye that sees through everything. As the leader of heaven, I reveal the path for people's lives. There is no need to panic when you get lost or lose your direction. When you are forced to stop by some obstacle, it is also a chance for realization. Take a good look at what it is saying.

付録
Appendix

●日本語索引（神名）

【あ】

足名椎神 あしなづちのかみ……22・56・58
阿比良比売 あひらひめ……106
天津麻羅 あまつまら……52
天照大御神 あまてらすおおみかみ……10・32・34・38・40・42・44・46・48・50・52・60・72・74・76・78・82・84・100
天宇受売命 あめのうずめのみこと……32・42・44・48・82・86
天児屋命 あめのこやねのみこと……44・46・48
天手力男神 あめのたぢからおのかみ……44・48
天之常立神 あめのとこたちのかみ……14・16
天之菩卑能命 あめのほひのみこと……74
天之御中主神 あめのみなかぬしのかみ……8・10

伊邪那岐命 いざなぎのみこと……18・20・22・24・28・30・32・34・36・54・76・104

伊邪那美命 いざなみのみこと……18・20・22・24・26・28・36・54・74

伊斯許理度売命 いしこりどめのみこと……44・50

市寸嶋比売命 いちきしまひめのみこと……38

石長比売 いわながひめ……22・90

宇迦之御魂神 うかのみたまのかみ……28

鵜葺草葺不合命 うがやふきあえずのみこと……96・98・100

海幸彦 うみさちひこ……92・94・102

上筒之男命 うわつつのおのみこと……30

上津綿津見神 うわつわたつみのかみ……104

大国主神 おおくにぬしのかみ……12・40・58・60・62・64・66・70・74・76・78・80

大宜都比売神 おおげつひめのかみ……54

大物主神 おおものぬしのかみ……106

大山津見神 おおやまつみのかみ……22・28・82・88

淤美豆奴神 おみずぬのかみ……70

思金神 おもいかねのかみ……40・44・82

【か】

神産巣日神 かみむすひのかみ……10・12・54・66

鹿屋野比売神 かやののひめのかみ……22

神倭伊波礼琵古命 かんやまといわれびこのみこと……98・100・102・106・108

草薙剣 くさなぎのつるぎ……84

櫛名田比売 くしなだひめ……36・56・58

奇魂 くしみたま……68

国之常立神 くにのとこたちのかみ……14・16

事代主神 ことしろぬしのかみ……78・80

木花之佐久夜毘売 このはなのさくやびめ……22・82・88・90・92

【さ】

幸魂 さきみたま……68

付録 | Appendix

猿田毗古神（さるたびこのかみ）……42・82・86
三種の神器（さんしゅのじんぎ）……48・82・84
塩椎神（しおつちのかみ）……92・100・102
神武天皇→神倭伊波礼毗古命（じんむてんのう・かんやまといわれびこのみこと）
綏靖天皇（すいぜいてんのう）……106
少名毗古那神（すくなびこなのかみ）……66
須勢理毗売命（すせりびめのみこと）……60・62・64
住吉三神（すみよしさんじん）……30・104
底筒之男命（そこつつのおのみこと）……30
底津綿津見神（そこわたつみのかみ）……104

【た】
高御産巣日神（たかみむすひのかみ）……10・12・40・48・82・108
当芸志美美命（たぎしみみのみこと）……106
多岐都比売命（たぎつひめのみこと）……38
多紀理毗売命（たきりびめのみこと）……38
建速須佐之男命（たけはやすさのおのみこと）……28・32・34・36・38・40・54・56・58・60・62・64・70・72・74・84
建比良鳥命（たけひらとりのみこと）……74
建御雷之男神（たけみかづちのおのかみ）……72・76・78・80
建御名方神（たけみなかたのかみ）……76・80
玉依毗売命（たまよりびめのみこと）……98・100・104
月読命（つくよみのみこと）……32・34・54
手名椎神（てなづちのかみ）……22・56・58
豊宇気神（とようけのかみ）……26
豊玉毗売命（とよたまびめのみこと）……92・96・98・104

【な】

中筒之男命 なかつつのおのみこと……30

中津綿津見神 なかつわたつみのかみ……104

邇邇芸命 ににぎのみこと……40・42・44・46・48・50・60・72・76・82・84・86・88・90・92・94

【は】

火之迦具土神 ひのかぐつちのかみ……20・24・26・76

経津主神 ふつぬしのかみ……80

布刀玉命 ふとだまのみこと……44・46・48・84

富登多多良伊須須岐比売命 ほとたたらいすすぎひめのみこと……106

【ま】

正勝吾勝勝速日天之忍穂耳命 まさかつあかつかちはやひめめのおしほみみのみこと……72・82

彌都波能売神 みずはのめのかみ……26

宗像三神 むなかたさんじん……38

【や】

八上比売 やがみひめ……60・62

八尺瓊勾玉 やさかにのまがたま……48・84

八咫烏 やたがらす……100・108

八尺鏡 やたのかがみ……48・50・84

山幸彦 やまさちひこ……92・94・96・98・100・102・104

【わ】

和久産巣日神 わくむすひのかみ……26

綿津見神 わたつみのかみ……30・92・94・96・98・102・104

●English Index (Names of Gods)

A
Ahirahime—107
Amaterasu—11,32,33,35,39,41,43,45,47,49,51,53,61,73, 75,77,79,83,85,101
Amatsumara—52,53
Amenohohi—74,75
Amenokoyane—45,46,47,49
Amenominakanushi—8,9,11
Amenooshihomimi—72,73,83
Amenotajikarao—44,45,49
Amenotokotachi—14,15,17
Amenouzume—33,42,43,45,49,83,87
Ashinazuchi—23,56,57,59

F
Futodama—45,47,48,49,85
Futsunushi—81

H
Hinokagutsuchi—21,24,25,27,77
Hototataraisusugihime—106,107

I
Ichikishimahime—39
Ishikoridome—45,50,51
Iwanagahime—23,90,91
Izanagi—18,19,21,23,25,29,31,33,35,37,55,77,105
Izanami—19,20,21,23,25,27,29,37,55,75

J
Jinmu—99,100,101,103,107,109

K
Kamimusuhi—11,12,13,55,67
Kanyamatoiwarebiko→Jinmu
Kayanohime—23
Konohananosakuyabime—23,83,88,89,91,93
Kotoshironushi—78,79,81
Kuninotokotachi—15,16,17
Kusanagino Tsurugi—85
Kushimitama—68,69
Kushinadahime—37,57,58,59

M
Mizuhanome—27
Munakatasanjin—38,39

N
Nakatsutsunoo—31
Nakawatatsumi—105
Ninigi—41,43,45,47,49,51,61,73,77,82,83,85,87,89,91,93,95

O
Omizunu—70,71
Omoikane—40,41,45,83
Oogetsuhime—54,55
Ookuninushi—13,41,59,60,61,63,65,67,71,75,77,79,81
Oomononushi—107
Ooyamatsumi—22,23,29,83,89

S

Sakimitama—68,69

Sanshunojingi—49,51,82,84,85

Sarutabiko—43,83,86,87

Shiotsuchi—93,101,102,103

Sokotsutsunoo—31

Sokowatatsumi—105

Suizei—107

Sukunabikona—66,67

Sumiyoshisanjin—30,31,105

Susanoo→Takehayasusanoo

Suseribime—61,63,64,65

T

Tagichuhime—39

Tagishimimi—107

Takamimusuhi—10,11,13,41,49,83,109

Takehayasusanoo—29,33,35,36,37,39,41,55,57,59,61,63,65,71,73,75,85

Takehiratori—75

Takemikazuchi—73,76,77,79,81

Takeminakata—77,80,81

Takiribime—39

Tamayoribime—98,99,101,105

Tenazuchi—23,56,57,59

Toyotamabime—93,96,97,99,105

Toyoukebime—27

Tsukuyomi—33,34,35,55

U

Ugayafukiaezu 97,99,101

Ukanomitama 28,29

Umisachihiko 93,94,95,103

Uwatsutsunoo 31

Uwawatatsumi 105

W

Wakumusuhi 26,27

Watatsumi 30,93,95,97,99,103,104,105

Y

Yagamihime 61,62,63

Yamasachihiko 92,93,95,97,99,101,103,105

Yasakanino Magatama 49,85

Yatagarasu 101,108,109

Yatano Kagami 49,51,85

系図 1 = 創世の神々
Relationship Diagram 1 "Gods who Created the Heavens and the Earth"

● 別天神 (ことあまつかみ) Kotoamatsukami

　● 造化三神 (ぞうかさんしん) Zoka sanshin
　　天之御中主神 (あめのみなかぬしのかみ) Amenominakanushi
　　高御産巣日神 (たかみむすひのかみ) Takamimusuhi
　　神産巣日神 (かみむすひのかみ) Kamimusuhi

　天之常立神 (あめのとこたちのかみ) Amenotokotachi
　宇摩志阿斯訶備比古遅神 (うましあしかびひこぢのかみ) Umashiashikabihikoji

● 神世七代 (かみよななよ)
　国之常立神 (くにのとこたちのかみ) Kuninotokotachi
　豊雲野神 (とよくもののかみ) Toyokumono
　宇比地邇神 (うひぢにのかみ) Uhijini ＝ 須比智邇神 (すひぢにのかみ) Suhijini
　角杙神 (つのぐいのかみ) Tunogui ＝ 活杙神 (いくぐいのかみ) Ikugui
　意富斗能地神 (おおとのぢのかみ) Ootonoji ＝ 大斗乃弁神 (おおとのべのかみ) Ootonobe
　於母陀流神 (おもだるのかみ) Omodaru ＝ 阿夜訶志古泥神 (あやかしこねのかみ) Ayakashikone
　伊邪那岐命 (いざなぎのみこと) Izanagi ＝ 伊邪那美命 (いざなみのみこと) Izanami

下線 ……… 性別の明らかでない神 Gender-Bending God
ゴチック体　　男神 Male God
明朝体 …… 女神 Female God
＝ ………　夫婦 Couple

- 水蛭子 Hiruko
- 志那都比古神 Shinatsuhiko
- 大山津見神 Ooyamatsumi
- 火之迦具土神 Hinokagutsuchi

- 泣澤女神 Nakisawame
- 住吉三神 Sumiyoshisanjin

- ●三貴子 Sankishi
  - 天照大御神 Amaterasu
  - 月読命 Tsukuyomi
  - 建速須佐之男命 Takehayasusanoo ＝ 神大市比売 Kamuooichihime
    - 大年神 Ootoshi
    - 宇迦之御魂神 Ukanomitama

- 金山毘古神 Kanayamabiko ＝ 金山毘売神 Kanayamabime
- 波邇夜須毘古神 Haniyasubiko ＝ 波邇夜須毘売神 Haniyasubime
- 和久産巣日神 Wakumusuhi ＝ 彌都波能売神 Mizuhanome

系図 2 = 高天原の神々
Relationship Diagram 2 "Gods of Takamanohara (The Plain of High Heaven)"

- **正勝吾勝勝速日天之忍穂耳命** Masakatsuakatsukachihayahiamenooshihomimi
  （まさかつあかつかちはやひあめのおしほみみのみこと）
- **天之菩卑能命** Amenohohi
  （あめのほひのみこと）
- **天津日子根命** Amatsuhikone
  （あまつひこねのみこと）
- **活津日子根命** Ikutsuhikone
  （いくつひこねのみこと）
- **熊野久須毘命** Kumanokusubi
  （くまのくすびのみこと）

下線 ………	性別の明らかでない神	Gender-Bending God
ゴチック体	男神	Male God
明朝体 ……	女神	Female God
＝ …………	夫婦	Couple

付録 | Appendix

```
いざなぎのみこと                いざなみのみこと
伊邪那岐命 Izanagi ══ 伊邪那美命 Izanami
   │
   │         おおげつひめのかみ
   │         大宜都比売神 Oogetsuhime
   │
   │  あまてらすおおみかみ
   ├─ 天照大御神 Amaterasu
   │  つくよみのみこと
   ├─ 月読命 Tsukuyomi
   │  たけはやすさのおのみこと
   └─ 建速須佐之男命 Takehayasusanoo
```

   ● 宗像三神 Munakatasanjin
      多紀理毘売命 Takiribime
      市寸嶋比売命 Ichikishimahime
      多岐都比売命 Tagitsuhime

● 天岩戸から天照大御神を出す Bring Amaterasu out of the Amano iwato

思金神 Omoikane　　　　　　　**布刀玉命** Futodama

天宇受売命 Amenouzume　　　**伊斯許理度売命** Ishikoridome

天手力男神 Amenotajikarao　　**天津麻羅** Amatsumara

天児屋命 Amenokoyane

```
伊邪那岐命 Izanagi ＝ 伊邪那美命 Izanami
                      │
                  大山津見神 Ooyamatsumi
                      │
        ┌─────────────┴─────────────┐
    足名椎神 Ashinazuchi ＝ 手名椎神 Tenazuchi
```

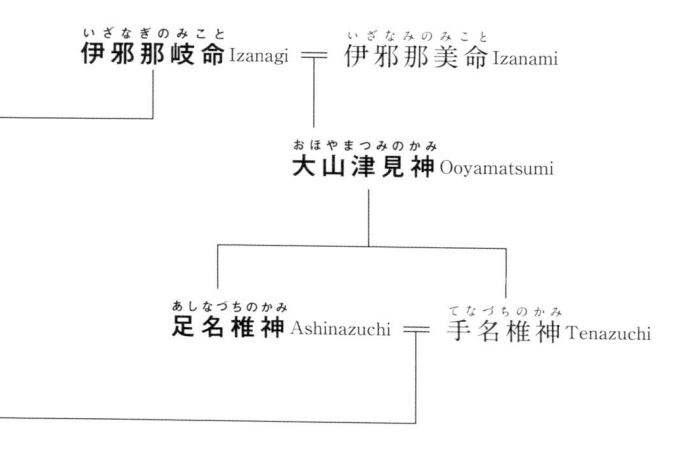

下線 ……… 性別の明らかでない神 Gender-Bending God
ゴチック体 男神 Male God
明朝体 …… 女神 Female God
＝ ………… 夫婦 Couple

付録 ― Appendix

系図3＝出雲の神々

Relationship Diagram 3 "Gods of Izumo"

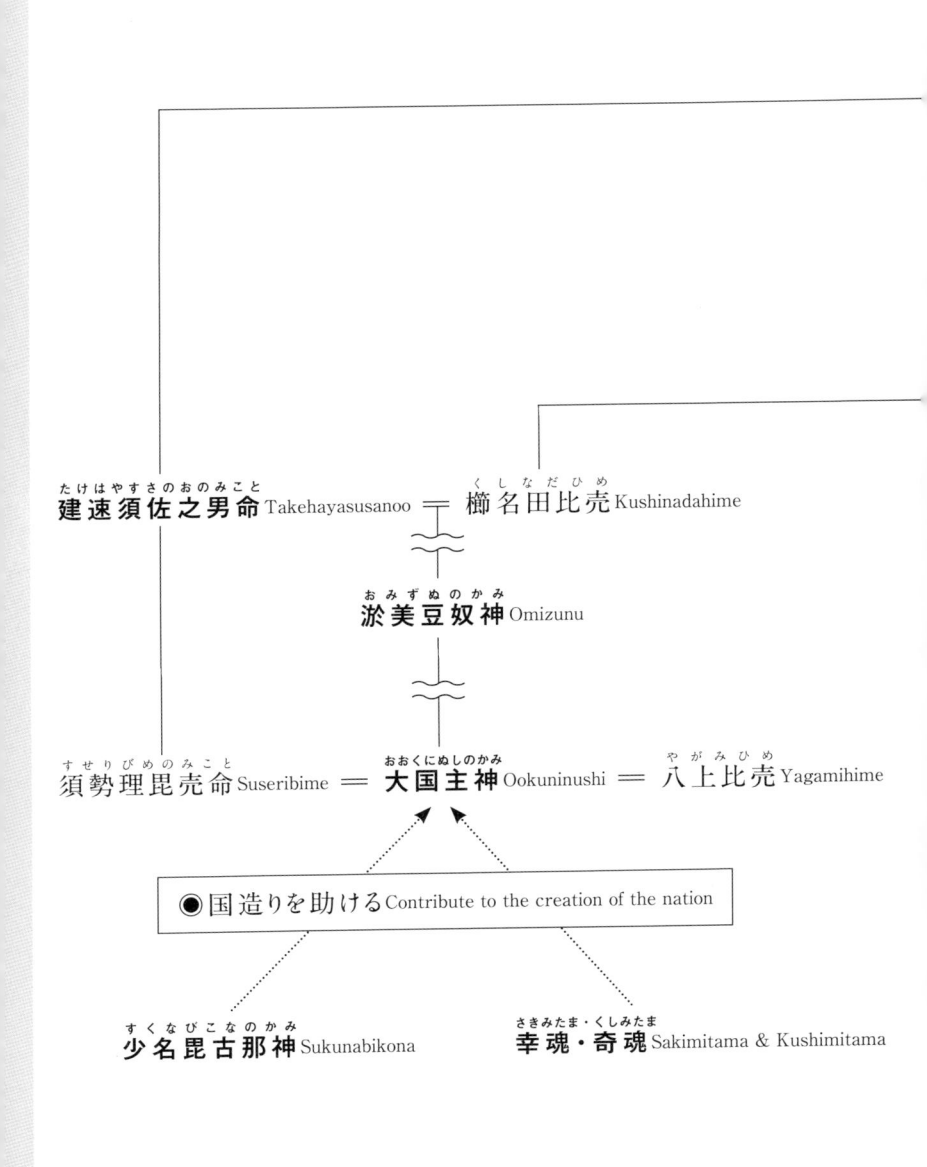

```
                    建速須佐之男命 Takehayasusanoo ═══ 櫛名田比売 Kushinadahime
                    たけはやすさのおのみこと            くしなだひめ
                                        │
                                   淤美豆奴神 Omizunu
                                    おみずぬのかみ
                                        │
     須勢理毘売命 Suseribime ═══ 大国主神 Ookuninushi ═══ 八上比売 Yagamihime
      すせりびめのみこと          おおくにぬしのかみ         やがみひめ
                           ▲    ▲
                           ┊    ┊
              ┌────────────┴────┴──────────────┐
              │ ●国造りを助ける Contribute to the creation of the nation │
              └──┬──────────────────────────┬──┘
                 ┊                          ┊
         少名毘古那神 Sukunabikona    幸魂・奇魂 Sakimitama & Kushimitama
          すくなびこなのかみ           さきみたま・くしみたま
```

系図4＝天孫降臨の神々

Relationship Diagram 4 "Gods of Tensonkorin(Went down to Earth with the Grandson of the Sun Goddess)"

- 伊邪那岐命 Izanagi ＝ 伊邪那美命 Izanami
  - 大山津見神 Ooyamatsumi
  - 火之迦具土神 Hinokagutsuchi
  - 建御雷之男神 Takemikazuchi
- 正勝吾勝勝速日天之忍穂耳命 Masakatsuakatsukachihayahiamenooshihomimi ‖ 万幡豊秋津師比売命 Yorozuhatatoyoakitsushihime
- 天之菩卑能命 Amenohohi
- 石長比売 Iwanagahime
- 木花之佐久夜毘売 Konohanasakuyabime ＝ 邇邇芸命 Ninigi

● 天孫降臨に同行した
Accompany Ninigi in the Tensonkorin

- 猿田毘古神 Sarutabiko ＝ 天宇受売命 Amenouzume
- 思金神 Omoikane
- 天手力男神 Amenotajikarao
- 天児屋命 Amenokoyane
- 布刀玉命 Hutodama
- 伊斯許理度売命 Ishikoridome

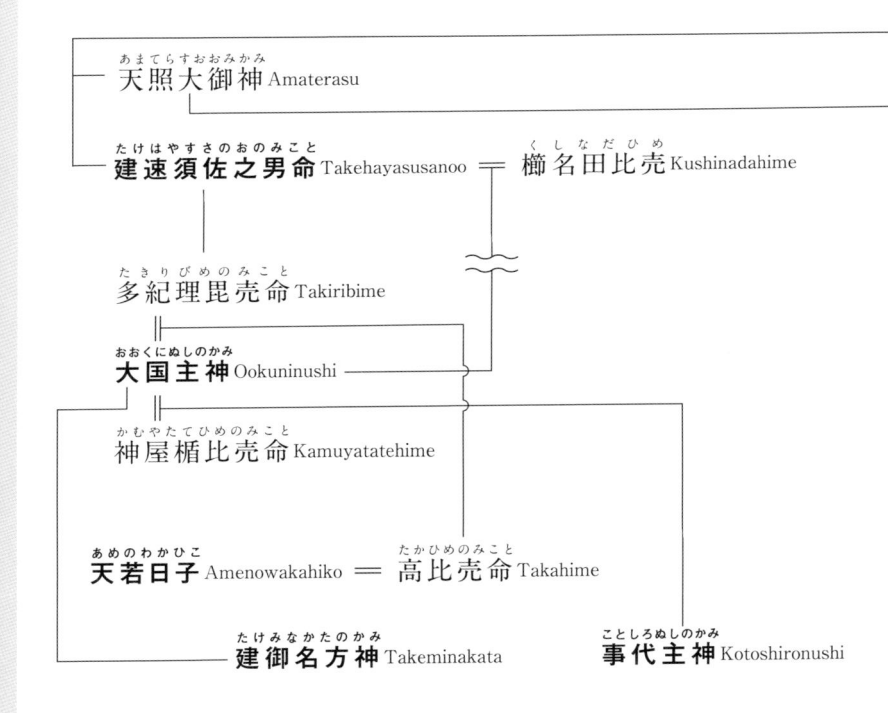

```
                                    あまてらすおおみかみ
                            ┌─── 天照大御神 Amaterasu
                            │
                            │      たけはやすさのおのみこと                    くしなだひめ
                            └─── 建速須佐之男命 Takehayasusanoo ══ 櫛名田比売 Kushinadahime
                                        │                              ╲╱
                                        │                              ╱╲
                                        │       たきりびめのみこと     ╲╱
                                        └── 多紀理毘売命 Takiribime
                                                    ‖
                                    おおくにぬしのかみ     │
                             ┌── 大国主神 Ookuninushi ────┤
                             │          ‖                │
                             │        かむやたてひめのみこと  │
                             │    神屋楯比売命 Kamuyatatehime
                             │                           │
                             │      あめのわかひこ            たかひめのみこと
                             │    天若日子 Amenowakahiko ══ 高比売命 Takahime
                             │
                             │              たけみなかたのかみ                  ことしろぬしのかみ
                             └──────── 建御名方神 Takeminakata      事代主神 Kotoshironushi
```

下線………	性別の明らかでない神 Gender-Bending God
ゴチック体	**男神** Male God
明朝体……	女神 Female God
══ ………	夫婦 Couple

系図5＝人皇誕生

Relationship Diagram 5 "The birth of the First Emperor"

付録｜Appendix

PAGE 126 / 127

邇邇芸命 Ninigi ＝ 木花之佐久夜毘売 Konohanasakuyabime

海幸彦 Umisachihiko

- 下線……… 性別の明らかでない神 Gender-Bending God
- ゴチック体　男神 Male God
- 明朝体…… 女神 Female God
- ＝………… 夫婦 Couple

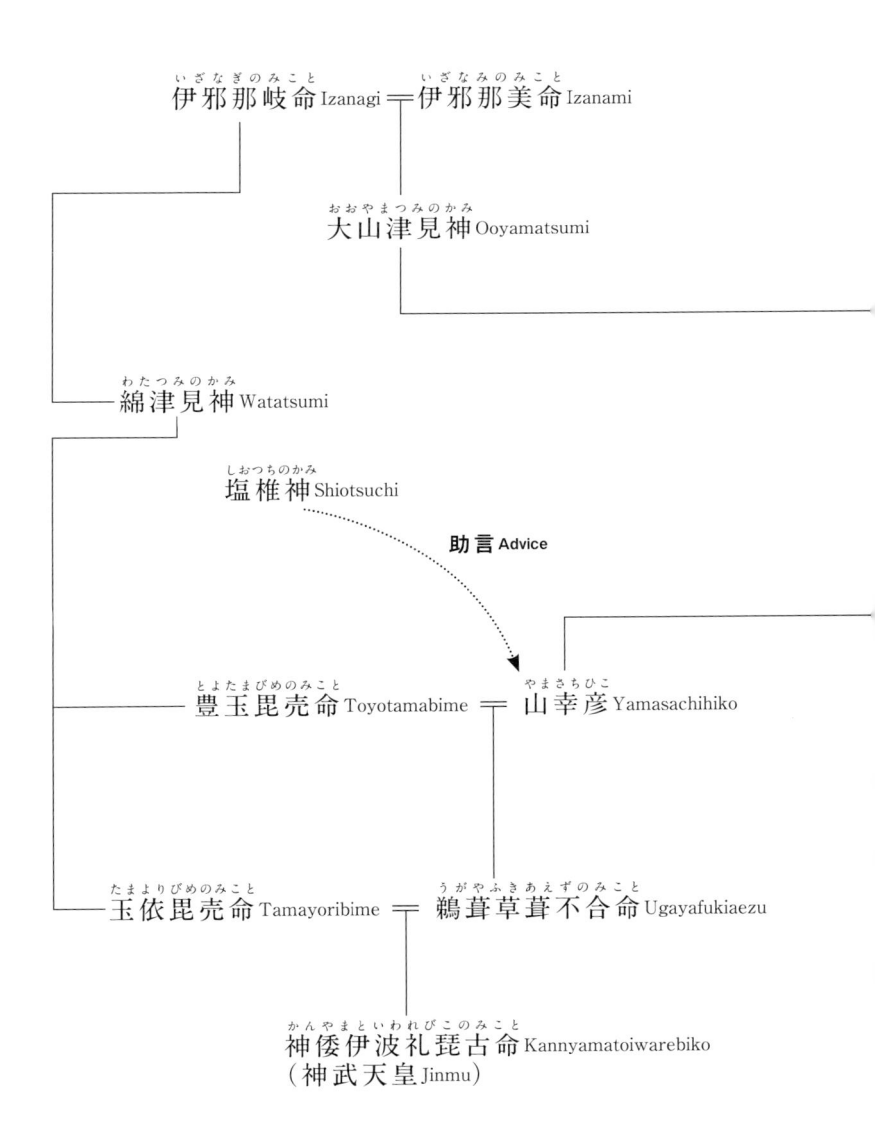

```
                伊邪那岐命 Izanagi ═ 伊邪那美命 Izanami
                                    │
                    ┌───────────────┤
                    │               │
                    │         大山津見神 Ooyamatsumi
                    │               │
                    │     ┌─────────┤
                    │     │         │
         ─ 綿津見神 Watatsumi        │
           │                        │
           │     塩椎神 Shiotsuchi   │
           │         ╲              │
           │          ╲  助言 Advice│
           │           ╲            │
           │            ╲→          │
           │                        │
        ─ 豊玉毘売命 Toyotamabime ═ 山幸彦 Yamasachihiko
           │                        │
           │                        │
        ─ 玉依毘売命 Tamayoribime ═ 鵜葺草葺不合命 Ugayafukiaezu
                    │
                    │
           神倭伊波礼琵古命 Kannyamatoiwarebiko
               （神武天皇 Jinmu）
```

日本の神様 Japanese Gods and Goddesses

2014年2月5日　初版第1刷　発行

著者　CR & LF 研究所
発行者　中川信行
発行所　株式会社マイナビ
　　　　〒100-0003 東京都千代田区一ツ橋1-1-1 パレスサイドビル
　　　　TEL：0480-485-2383（注文専用ダイヤル）
　　　　TEL：03-6267-4477（販売部）TEL：03-6267-4445（編集部）
　　　　E-mail：pc-books@mynavi.jp　URL：http://book.mynavi.jp
印刷・製本　株式会社大丸グラフィックス

【注意事項について】
○本書の一部または全部について個人で使用するほかは、著作権上、著作権者および(株)マイナビの承諾を得ずに無断で複写、複製することは禁じられております。
○本書についてのご質問等がございましたら、右記メールアドレスにお問い合わせください。インターネット環境のない方は、往復はがきまたは返信用切手、返信用封筒を同封の上、(株)マイナビ出版事業本部編集第6部書籍編集1課までお送りください。
○乱丁・落丁についてのお問い合わせは、TEL：0480-485-2383（注文専用ダイヤル）、電子メール：sas@mynavi.jpまでお願いいたします。
○本書中の会社名、商品名は、該当する会社の商標または登録商標です。
定価はカバーに記載しております。

©Creative Room & Life Facilitation lab. 2014. ©Mynavi Corporation 2014. All rights reserved. ISBN978-4-8399-4966-2
Printed in Japan

● 著者…CR & LF 研究所

● イラスト…中川 学

● ブックデザイン…Variant design

● 執筆…津久井孝江＜月音＞
高橋祐子、前田有香（CR & LF研究所）

● 翻訳…飯田ひろみ

● 英文校正…ビーコス

● 企画・編集
成田晴香、山本雅之（マイナビ）

● Author
Creative Room & Life Facilitation lab.

● Illust
Gaku Nakagawa

● Design
Variant design

● Writing
=TSUKINE=TaKae Tsukui,
Yuko Takahashi,
Yuka Maeda
(Creative Room & Life Facilitation lab.)

● Translation
Hiromi Iida

● English Proofreading
b-cause co,. Inc

● Planner, Editor
Haruka Narita, Masayuki Yamamoto
(Mynavi Corporation)